The Simple Guide to
Thesis Statements
and Support

The Simple Guide to Thesis Statements and Support

Patricia Martin MA MEd

 On Demand Instruction

The Simple Guide to Thesis Statements and Support

Table of Contents

Preface

Are you writing a paper and confused by your teacher's instruction? Do you want to help your teenager with a school essay but feel lost as to what advice to give? Are you returning to school yourself, after years away, and find that first essay assignment overwhelming? Is there a local or state issue that you need to write a legislature about but are uncertain of how to structure your thoughts?

Everyone runs into these situations at some point. People need to know how to state their viewpoints, how to support their views and how to present information properly. Considering that the writing process takes most writers years to perfect, it is common for teenagers and professional adults alike to struggle with writing.

Few writers are masterful essayists when they start out. Writing and supporting a strong thesis statement takes time and practice. Many writers struggle with constructing a thesis and how to support one with valid information. Thesis statements (theses) are probably the most challenging elements of essay writing. In this book, we attempt to present the crafting of thesis statements and their support in a simple, straightforward manner.

Think that thesis statements are only for high school essays? Think again.

Citizens who write letters to government representatives use thesis statements to voice their opinions and use facts and evidence to support them. Consumers reach out to businesses to suggest product improvements and make requests. Business professionals communicate in memos, emails and letters to colleagues and other businesses about products and services, and they use thesis statements to make their points.

Like all of the books in the Simple Guide Books series, *The Simple Guide to Thesis Statements and Support* is written for the person who may struggle with this topic and the person who needs basic explanations with straightforward examples. The book helps students, parents and professionals alike to achieve their goals of improving their writing.

All writers encounter thesis statements and support at some point. Student writers, from elementary school through graduate levels, compose and defend thesis statements in essays. As well, workers in every profession write thesis statements for a variety of purposes.

What is a Thesis Statement?

What is a Thesis Statement

A thesis statement is the strong arguable opinion the writer attempts to prove in an essay, short answer, research paper, letter or other piece of writing.

The thesis statement is the entire purpose to an essay or research paper; without it, there is no direction to the paper. The thesis statement will hold together all of the information, facts, quotations and suggestions within an essay. It is what the reader should be learning about while reading the piece of writing.

Think of an essay's content like a pyramid. When tourists go to visit a pyramid, they do not gaze with amazement at the base but rather at the pinnacle—the very highest point of the structure. An essay's ideas are the same. The thesis is at the very top. This is where the readers look to find the most important information; the thesis is the one sentence that the whole paper is about. Everything under that pinnacle supports it. Just as in a pyramid, all of the lower stones hold up the pinnacle, in an essay all of the data, facts, statistics, examples and quotations hold up the thesis; they support the thesis.

Infographic: What is a Thesis Statement

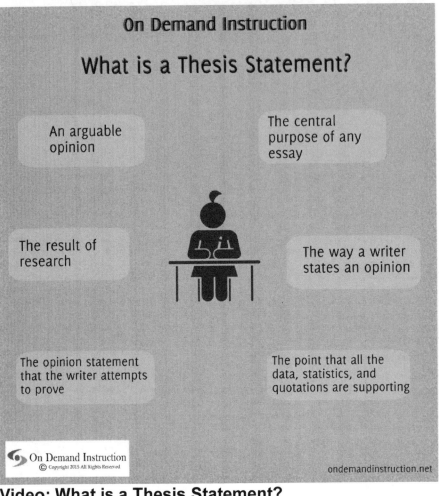

On Demand Instruction

What is a Thesis Statement?

An arguable opinion

The central purpose of any essay

The result of research

The way a writer states an opinion

The opinion statement that the writer attempts to prove

The point that all the data, statistics, and quotations are supporting

On Demand Instruction
© Copyright 2015 All Rights Reserved

ondemandinstruction.net

Video: What is a Thesis Statement?

http://wp.me/P2xgad-bk

What Are Other Terms For a Thesis?

A thesis statement goes by many names. Some people will use the terms: proposition statement, opinion statement, argument, standpoint, viewpoint, controlling idea, unifying statement, main idea, analysis statement, topic sentence, central argument or any number of terms that may be added to this list.

Is there any problem with people using different terms for thesis statements? Not at all. Sometimes, a teacher or editor is dedicated to using a particular term because it communicates more clearly for that person. Be aware that different people use different terms, though the meaning and purpose are the same.

The most common term is *thesis statement*, which will be used throughout this book. Do not be alarmed when hearing another term used in a classroom or writing setting; this is not unusual and the person will be using the term with the same meaning—an arguable viewpoint.

As well, different writing programs will focus on a particular term to emphasize some particular aspect of it; this should not cause a problem as long as writers realize that the function of the thesis statement is the same, regardless of what it is called.

A thesis statement is not a fact or a factual statement. It is not a weak or an uncertain statement. It is not a question or a rhetorical statement. A thesis statement is a strong arguable opinion that a writer uses in writing.

How is a Thesis Statement Used?

A thesis statement is used to organize, focus and direct an essay, short answer or research paper. The writer uses the thesis statement to give the reader a clear idea of what the piece of writing covers. Writers do this by stating which viewpoints they will attempt to prove in the paper.

The thesis statement is the central point of the entire piece of writing, regardless if that is a one-paragraph memo or a two-hundred page book. Writers can wield incredible power by how they phrase a thesis. A thesis can be expository, persuasive or narrative. Regardless of the type of writing, a thesis statement is always the main focus of any piece of writing. It is what is being proven in the paper and the sentence that is supported by the examples, evidence and data.

Infographic: Thesis Statement

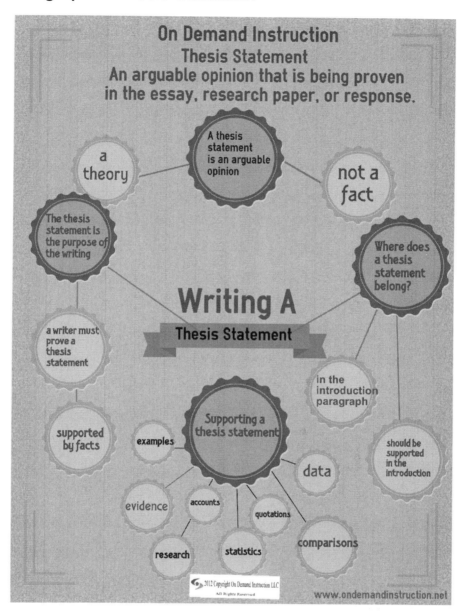

On Demand Instruction
Thesis Statement
An arguable opinion that is being proven in the essay, research paper, or response.

a theory

A thesis statement is an arguable opinion

not a fact

The thesis statement is the purpose of the writing

Where does a thesis statement belong?

Writing A

Thesis Statement

a writer must prove a thesis statement

in the introduction paragraph

supported by facts

examples

Supporting a thesis statement

data

should be supported in the introduction

evidence

accounts

quotations

research

statistics

comparisons

2012 Copyright On Demand Instruction LLC
All Rights Reserved

www.ondemandinstruction.net

17

Thesis Statements

in

Quick Writing

Thesis Statements in Quick Writing

An assignment's writing prompt impels the writer to answer a question by stating an opinion. That opinion becomes the thesis statement for the paper.

For example, imagine that a teacher gives a writing prompt that says, "Defend your viewpoint about a national issue." The writer might choose the rising costs of college, changes in the economy, expansion of renewable energy or some other topic. Because the prompt suggests using a personal opinion, the writer will not conduct research. Instead, the writer is most likely to write a thesis statement, then collect and organize support from memory.

This method is useful for timed writing tasks, especially on standardized tests, interview questions or when meeting a short deadline. Since people who are taking a standardized test cannot conduct research, they need to be able to write a thesis statement and defend it quickly.

Not only is this a useful skill for timed writing and testing situations, but quick writing is for people working in jobs that require speedy thinking and decision making. Being able to think and write quickly as well as to defend one's opinions can be the difference between failure and success for some situations.

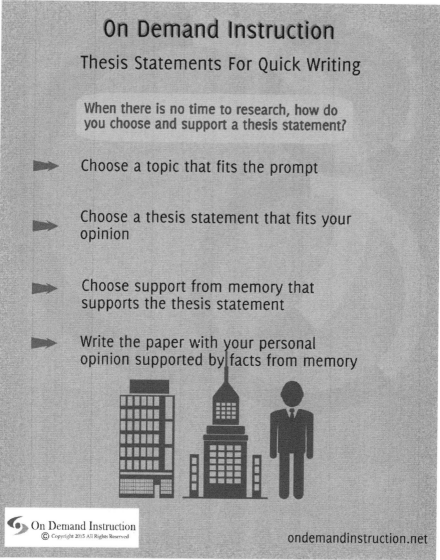

On Demand Instruction
Thesis Statements For Quick Writing

When there is no time to research, how do you choose and support a thesis statement?

➡ Choose a topic that fits the prompt

➡ Choose a thesis statement that fits your opinion

➡ Choose support from memory that supports the thesis statement

➡ Write the paper with your personal opinion supported by facts from memory

On Demand Instruction
© Copyright 2015 All Rights Reserved

ondemandinstruction.net

Video: Quick Writing

http://wp.me/P2xgad-bo

Example Prompts

What are examples of writing prompts that may require a quickly-written thesis statement and support?

- State your opinion about public school funding and defend it.
- Defend a viewpoint on the ways that America's national parks could be best managed.
- Explain what it means to be a hero in modern society.

With any of these prompts, a writer needs to declare the thesis statement and defend it right away. If the situation calls for an immediate response, then the writer should write the thesis and defend it without research.

Although the quick write has its limitations, writers need to be able to use it, while being aware of its restrictions. The drawbacks to this method include: less learning is occurring, writers are defending what they already know or believe and less depth and breadth of information may be included in this writing style.

The shortcomings in quick writing are:

- The writer is not learning about the topic beyond existing knowledge.
- The writer is not challenging his/her current thoughts.

- The writer is not growing and expanding his/her knowledge on the topic.
- The writer's viewpoint may be wrong, but without conducting research, there is little opportunity to find that out.
- The essay will only include the information the writer knows.
- The writing may be shallow or contain outdated information.

The reality is that this method must be used at times, even though it does have some drawbacks. Since sometimes there is no opportunity to conduct research, writers need to be able to pose and defend opinions quickly. This can happen in writing and speaking situations. Although the quick writing method has its drawbacks, writers who can pose and defend a thesis quickly and without research are more flexible than those who are limited to using an extended writing process.

Imagine that a person is in a job interview and is asked, "What is the most important skill for managers to have and why?" In this situation, the person being interviewed needs to answer and defend the viewpoint with examples but without referencing any researched sources.

The same is true of a timed-writing sample. When asked to respond to the prompt, "Explain the most important value to teach young children," writers will not have the luxury of researching. Instead, readers expect a strong, thorough and quick answer.

This method of stating and defending an opinion is limited when compared to using the full extended writing process, which allows for research, interviews and data collection. But since there are so many uses for quick thinking, speaking and writing, competent communicators need to practice this skill to be able to perform it well. The person who is able to write, think and speak quickly demonstrates a great advantage over the person who cannot be so efficient. If this method is new, give it a try. Work through a few prompts without allowing for research and data-collection time. Forcing oneself to practice writing without research and within a time limit can hone skills in writing and supporting thesis statements.

Practice Prompts

- What dietary change should most Americans make to improve their health?
- State an opinion about the upcoming election and defend it.
- What lesson is most important for modern children to learn and why?

Thesis Statements

in

Extended Writing

Thesis Statements in Extended Writing

In extended writing, the writer does not need to deliver an immediate response. Instead, time is available to research, reflect and compose a more in-depth piece of writing.

A research question (typically as part of a research process) impels the writer to conduct research; then after reviewing the available literature, the writer constructs the thesis statement to communicate the outcome of the research. The thesis statement is the result of the research not the motivation for the research.

For example, when a writer is conducting an investigation, starting with a research question is typically the best method. A writer might do this for a school assignment or a professional task. It may be personal curiosity that drives the inquiry.

A writing prompt that impels a writer to conduct research prior to writing the thesis statement might state, "Research a local initiative to improve people's health and report on its effects."

In this scenario, writers would locate a local health initiative (perhaps a program to label genetically-modified foods or change public school lunch menus), collect the available research supporting a variety of viewpoints on the topic and then construct the thesis statement around these findings. The research comes before the thesis statement.

This method is more scientific than the quick write method since the research of facts trumps opinion in validity. Need an example? In 1996, the FBI suspected security guard Richard Jewell of setting off a bomb at the Olympics in Georgia; this was because the FBI conducted poor research. Later, after a properly-conducted investigation, the FBI found that Jewell was actually the hero not the bomber. Researching prior to composing the thesis matters.

In the extended-writing scenario, the writer poses a research question or hypothesis before conducting the research.

These steps would include:

1. Pose a research question or hypothesis
2. Research the various potential answers to the research question
3. Construct a thesis statement based on the outcome of the research.

The original research question drives the research forward. With the question open, the writer seeks out potential answers and facts related to the question. The thesis statement comes out of the research and the conclusions which the writer derives from it.

Infographic: Thesis Statements for Research

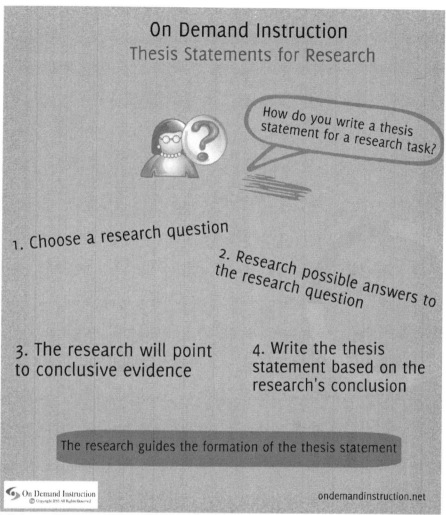

Video: Theses for Extended Writing

http://wp.me/P2xgad-bq

Example

Imagine that the writing prompt reads, "Ask a research question on voter registration laws and report out on your findings."

The question might read, "What voter registration laws have been passed recently and with what results?"

Now the writer has a focus and can investigate this topic of voter registration laws and their results.

Imagine that the research concluded with these findings:

- New laws in 2014 regarding voter registration included laws in Texas, Wisconsin and Virginia requiring all voters to provide a state-issued ID to vote.
- Those supporting the laws suggest the laws stop fraudulent voting.
- Those against the laws purport the laws stop minority and poor people from voting.
- Lawsuits have challenged the laws.

With results from the research on this topic, a writer might support these thesis statements:

1. Although unpopular in minority neighborhoods, requiring all voters to prove their identities with valid, state identification lowers the likelihood of voter fraud.

Or

2. Even though laws passed to lessen voter fraud require state identification, they also disenfranchise millions of minority and poor voters across America.

Depending upon the outcome of the investigation, either thesis statement may work well for this topic.

The importance here is that the thesis statement is constructed as a result of the research not the other way around. This is similar to the process that a scientist uses when posing a hypothesis, conducting an inquiry around the hypothesis and reporting the findings. The thesis statement is not constructed until the end.

Another consideration to thesis statement construction has to do with the facts. If a writer depends solely on personal opinion for the thesis support, then there is no opportunity for growth or learning. The writer defends personal opinions without consulting new information on the subject.

When a writer asks a new research question and conducts up-to-date research, then the information provided and the thesis that comes out of it is the most recent and relevant. This is the difference between writers depending on opinions and doing their research before writing.

Prompts

and

Responding to Them

Prompts and Responding to Them

Writers are frequently asked to respond to a writing prompt in class assessments, standardized tests and in writer's groups.

A prompt gives the writer a topic. Teachers use prompts to assess students' abilities and content knowledge. Employers use prompts to determine a candidate's likelihood to fit into a team. Facilitators use writing prompts to encourage writers to try out new content or styles.

A writer uses the writing prompt as the task's instructions and should refer back to the prompt throughout the writing process. This is because some writers may veer off topic and wander into a loosely-related idea, but referring back to the prompt throughout the process limits this likelihood to get off task.

Responding to a writing prompt is a learned skill that most writers need to practice. At first, some writers may feel like responding to a writing prompt is a slow process, but over time, most writers speed up and are eventually able to respond to prompts proficiently.

Infographic: How to Address a Prompt

On Demand Instruction

How to Address a Prompt

Read the prompt.

Make sure that you understand all parts. Are there several steps?
Put things into order. How will you go about answering it?

Reread it and <u>underline</u> or highlight key words.

Go through and read it again, more carefully this time, picking up what
you missed before. Underline key words and concepts. This is a good
time to get things clarified before you move on.

Analyze the content.

Determine what kinds of materials, texts, and ideas you will need to address
in this assignment. Do you have older materials that you can use as sources?
Or will you need to find new materials?

Beware of prompts with multiple steps.

Make sure you answer ALL parts of the prompt. If it asks you to write 3 paragraphs,
don't turn in 3 sentences.
How long should it be?
What needs to be included?
Do you understand every part?

www.OnDemandInstruction.net

Video: How to Respond to Writing Prompts

http://wp.me/P2xgad-bu

Example

A quiz or exam, either in class or on a standardized test, may contain prompts similar to these:

- Explain why scientists believe that climate change is having effects on the earth.
- Defend an opinion about why some children learn better in online classes.
- Contrast two viewpoints on the minimum wage debate.

Likewise, while working with a writing group, writers oftentimes practice their craft by writing responses to different prompts. This allows writers to practice with different styles and work with elements like tone, style and organization in different ways.

Example

A writing group might pose writing prompts similar to these:

- Compose a letter asking advice from your favorite author and include a piece of your own in-progress writing.

- Imitate the writing style of Poe, Hemingway or O'Connor when composing a narrative.
- Draft a persuasive proposal letter to the editor of *The New Yorker* suggesting that your newest story be considered for publication.

Rephrasing Prompts

A writing prompt can be rephrased into either a hook statement or into a thesis statement for certain situations. This works well for short answers and essays that are timed or quick writing.

The thesis statement is the arguable opinion which the whole paper supports. The hook or catch statement is before the thesis and *hooks* the reader to *catch* the reader's attention. The hook might be constructed as: a rhetorical question, an interesting statistic, a brief story, a quotation or an anecdote.

To rephrase a writing prompt means to take the key words within it and use those in a new statement. Only the key words are used; do not use every word from the prompt in the new statement. Instead, just use the most important words or phrases in the reworded statement.

Example

Prompt: Discuss three causes for the American Civil War.

Rephrased Statement: Three causes for the American Civil War included slavery, differing economic policies and transportation development.

In the example above, the writer uses the phrase, "Three causes for the American Civil War" directly from the writing prompt in the rephrased statement. Since this new statement is an opinion statement, it can be used as a thesis statement.

Example

Prompt: In a short response, analyze why organization is important in business letters.

Rephrased Statement: Organization is important in business letters, because writers want to communicate a point concisely and clearly.

In the second example, the length of writing is specified as a short answer, but this does not change the way that the prompt is rephrased into a new statement. The phrase "organization is important in business letters" is kept identical in the rephrased statement. Only the important words are used in the rephrased statement. This method can make quick work of writing thesis statements or hook statements. Once those are in place, the rest of the writing tends to come together easily.

Constructing

a

Thesis Statement

Constructing a Thesis Statement

Just as there are a dozen different names for a thesis statement, there are a dozen different ways to construct a thesis statement. Some teachers or editors may be dedicated to a particular style of thesis statement and if that is the case, then appease them as needed to reach your personal goal of a grade or a publishing opportunity.

Regardless of which method you choose for constructing your thesis statement, the most important aspect to remember is that the thesis statement must be an arguable opinion; it states what the writer will attempt to prove within the piece.

Basic Thesis Statements for Novice Writers

Young writers begin constructing short answers and basic essays in elementary school. It is typical for a third grader to be capable of writing a short response. Some young writers are able to express their opinions easily and others find the task overwhelming. A trick that can make the process easier for novice writers is to use--I think, I feel, or I believe--at the beginning of their thesis statements.

For writers who feel overwhelmed by expository writing, starting out with a basic thesis statement can be a comfortable beginning point. When a writer masters the basic thesis statement, he or she can move into one of the more sophisticated styles mentioned below. In the basic thesis statement, begin with one of the three following phrases:

- I think
- I feel
- I believe

By opening with one of these phrases, the novice writer has a natural start to writing an opinion. The rest of the sentence tends to flow smoothly once the initial phrase is on paper.

Examples

I think that school lunches should be made with all organic, fresh ingredients to promote good health.

I feel that school lunches give children the wrong message about healthy eating by serving pizza and corn dogs.

I believe that school lunches tend to be unhealthy and lead to poor eating habits in children.

After the writer is comfortable stating an opinion, just remove the words, I think, I feel, or I believe, and the thesis statement will be stronger.

a. I think that *The Hobbit* is an interesting fantasy book with a strong theme of adventure.

Later on, challenge the novice writer to remove the phrase "I think" and the result looks like this.

b. *The Hobbit* is an interesting fantasy book with a strong theme of adventure.

In basic theses, the novice writer enjoys some assistance in writing the thesis statement with the "I think" phrase, then in the second, the writer improves upon the thesis by removing the phrase.

Each of the three phrases will bring different connotations with them, which can allow young writers an opportunity to choose which phrase best suits their writing needs of the moment (thinking, feeling or believing).

a. I feel that kids should have more time outdoors during the school day for exercise and fresh air.

Later on, the student may remove the emotional phrase, "I feel".

b. Kids should have more time outdoors during the school day for exercise and fresh air.

a. I believe that dogs are much better pets than cats for kids of all ages.

Later on, the student may remove the faith statement, "I believe".

b. Dogs are much better pets than cats for kids of all ages.

Constructing strong thesis statements is a process that a writer perfects over time. Starting out with smaller steps can make the goals more easily attainable and increase the writer's engagement with expository writing.

Infographic: Basic Thesis Statements

On Demand Instruction
Basic Thesis Statements

I THINK   I FEEL   I BELIEVE

I THINK
I think that the Denver Broncos are the best football team ever.
I think that all children should be required to have vaccines.
I think dogs make better pets than cats do.

I FEEL
I feel that all families should get free preschool.
I feel that two weeks of vacation is not enough time
to stay healthy.
I feel that reading is the best past time for teenagers.

I BELIEVE
I believe that the driving age should be raised to 18.
I believe that towns should provide housing and mental health
services for the homeless.
I believe that cell phone are responsible for some cancers.

On Demand Instruction
© Copyright 2015 All Rights Reserved

ondemandinstruction.net

Video: Basic Thesis Statements

http://wp.me/P2xgad-bx

Sophisticated Thesis Statements

Many novice writers tend to be uncomfortable when constructing their first thesis statements and essays. They take more time in the writing process and in generating ideas. When stating and defending a viewpoint, writers can sometimes feel like the process is overwhelming.

Over time, this changes. Once writers have composed a few thesis statements, the process speeds up. After creating a few essays with strong thesis statements and different types of support, writers feel more comfortable with the process. When it comes to the writing process, practice makes for better writing; keep practicing to keep improving.

Writers should transition into sophisticated thesis statement forms after the basic thesis statement becomes easy to construct. A sophisticated thesis will come across at a higher level of thinking. It will have a more professional presentation and a more academic tone. The writing improves in all areas-tone, voice, vocabulary and presentation-when the writer uses a sophisticated thesis.

In the classroom setting, a young writer might spend a few months or even a year practicing the basic thesis before attempting a sophisticated form. Whereas, an adult writer might only need a couple of days or perhaps weeks before being ready to try to ratchet up their thesis quality.

Either way, shifting into the sophisticated thesis improves the writer and the writing.

Once writers have transitioned from the basic thesis to the sophisticated thesis statement, writers typically change their focus away from how to format a thesis to how to improve it with professional-level vocabulary. The sophisticated thesis statement formats explained in this book can be used for high school and college essays, including graduate school essays. As well, writers can use these formats for professional purposes like letter writing and professional reports. The formats are universal and work well for many different settings.

Infographic: Sophisticated Thesis Statements

On Demand Instruction
Sophisticated Thesis Statements

Why and What Thesis Statements

When the company can save 20% per year by going green, we need to make environmentally-friendly changes immediately.

Beginning With Data

Since food prices have risen sharply over the last year but wages have not, more local measures are necessary to address hunger.

Acknowledging the Opposition

Although some may disagree, protecting the right to garden in cities is an important issue to protect.

Video: Sophisticated Thesis Statements

http://wp.me/P2xgad-bA

Why and What Thesis

Once writers have perfected the basic thesis statement they can move into more interesting methods for stating opinions. The why and what thesis is a method that gives writers a strong tool to use in thesis writing.

Tell your reader why you are trying to prove the thesis and what the thesis is. This gives the reader a reason to continue reading.

Example

When vaccinations cut down on communicable diseases and child mortality, public schools should require vaccination records for all students.

In the example above, the writer includes a reason or *why* at the beginning: When vaccinations cut down on communicable diseases and child mortality. The opinion or *what* within the writing is: public schools should require vaccination records for all students. The reader should be engaged in the piece from the start.

Beginning with Data

When a writer begins a thesis statement with data, statistics or strong facts, the actual opinion is preceded by support. The reader is compelled to follow the thesis and engage with the writing.

Data is powerful for many readers because it gives mathematical information as the base of the argument. Using data shows the reader that the thesis statement is the result of research. It also shows the reader that the writer is taking a professional stance in presenting the essay's information.

Example

Since a recent study showed that more than a third of all adolescents were overweight, and since weight issues lead to diseases, Americans should make following a healthy lifestyle their highest priority.

Acknowledging the Opposition

Another useful method for constructing a thesis statement is to begin with an acknowledgement of the opposing viewpoint. Since all thesis statements give an opinion, there will always be an opposing viewpoint. Writers can use that to an advantage by acknowledging the opposition first. This demonstrates a depth of thought and suggests that the opposing viewpoint will be proven false.

Example

Although some people believe that the traditional high school should work for all students, most teenagers perform better and enjoy their education more at an online program.

In the example above, the writer is questioning the traditional high school model. The writer suggests that the majority of students would prefer another school model, which replaces the viewpoint that all students perform well at a traditional school. By suggesting that the traditional high school model does not meet the needs of the majority of students, the writer sets up for a strong thesis.

Expectations

for

Written Pieces

Expectations for Written Pieces

Depending on the situation, course, teacher, purpose and audience, different expectations exist for different writing tasks. In a classroom situation, students write short answers, essays, research papers, narratives and professional pieces to demonstrate their learning.

In a professional situation, workers compose different types of writing depending on the purpose and audience. Regardless if a person is writing for the classroom or the boardroom, there are always expectations for the writing: its format, length, formality, complexity and content.

Sometimes, novice writers are unsure of what questions to ask with regard to writing expectations. Here are some that may help:

- How formal should the writing be?
- Who is the audience?
- What is the writing purpose?
- Should the piece be expository, persuasive or some other form?
- How long should the piece be?

- Does the piece require research? If so, what research method (MLA, APA, AP, Chicago) should be used?

Infographic: Different Writing Styles

On Demand Instruction

Different Writing Styles

Writing can seem intimidating. In fact, it can actually be quite simple if you approach it the right way.

First, you have to know what style of writing you will compose.

Narrative Writing

Tell a story
Real-life experience
Involve the reader
Make it as vivid as possible
Engage the reader
Write in first person
Build toward drawing a conclusion
or making a personal statement

Comparison or Contrast Writing

Show how two things are
similar
OR
Show how two things are
different
Anecdotes
Comparative data
Shared statistics
Charts and graphs
Survey results
Compare professional
opinions

Expository Writing

Informative
Gives just the facts
Present a balanced analysis
Explain or define a topic
Use facts, statistics, and
examples
Basis in fact, not opinion
or emotion
Don't write in first person
Can be many types of essay,
such as compare/contrast,
cause/effect, or how-to

Persuasive Writing

Convince the reader to accept
your point of view
Build a case using facts and
logic
Give examples, expert opinion,
and sound reasoning
Present all sides of the
argument
Communicate clearly without
doubt or question why their
position is correct

 2012 Copyright On Demand Instruction LLC

All Rights Reserved

www.OnDemandInstruction.net

Short Responses

Sometimes, young people think that what they are learning in the classroom does not translate to the professional world or *real world* as some people call it. However, everything that is taught for writing has a purpose in the workaday world, although it may go by a different name.

Short answers or short responses are used in school and work. A short answer in the classroom is a one to three paragraph response to a prompt. Students typically run across short responses on book reflections, content reviews, quizzes and exams. Writing shorter than an essay is called a short answer or a short response for students.

In the professional world, a short response is used in professional memos, interoffice communications and professional emails. If a business partner emails wanting a brief response, a short response should do the trick. If a colleague asks a question about a new product, replying with a short response should include the correct amount of information.

How is a Short Response Constructed?

A short response contains a thesis statement, support and a conclusion. Just as in an essay, the short response begins with the introduction paragraph (hook statements, thesis statement, three to seven broad, general support statements and a conclusion statement). If the full response is only one paragraph long, this should be enough information.

When writing a short response that is longer than one paragraph, include a one paragraph introduction and two to three body paragraphs.

The introduction paragraph should include:

- One to two hook statements
- A thesis statement
- Three to seven broad, general support statements
- A conclusion statement

The body paragraphs (or support paragraphs) are dedicated to providing support, evidence, data and statistics that prove the thesis statement is correct.

The body paragraphs are each constructed with:

- An introduction sentence
- Three to seven support statements that contain evidence, data and statistics which support the thesis statement
- A conclusion statement

The result is a short response where all of the information supports the thesis statement. Since a thesis statement is an arguable opinion, it needs facts, data and statistics to demonstrate that it is correct. Teachers, from elementary school through college, use short responses for a variety of assessment purposes.

Since a short answer is such a concise piece of writing, the thesis statement is often softer and narrower than theses used for longer pieces. When writing a short answer, take into consideration that there will only be a brief opportunity to discuss the topic, so a more narrow topic and thesis works better. In longer pieces, like essays, research papers and even books, a broader and more complicated thesis works well. Over time, writers improve their abilities of writing thesis statements that work for different styles and lengths of writing.

Infographic: Short Response

On Demand Instruction

Short Response

What is a short response?

A short answer response requires the student to answer a specific question, usually in 1-3 paragraphs.

How to compose

Read the prompt all the way through before you answer.

Make sure you understand what it is asking.

Answer all parts of the prompt and follow directions. If it asks multiple questions, be sure to answer them all.

Use a variety of sentence lengths and types.

Use standard English and proofread your work carefully before you turn it in.

Your response should be 1-3 paragraphs, and each paragraph should be at least 5 sentences long.

If you have questions, ask before responding.

www.OnDemandInstruction.net

Video: The Short Response

http://wp.me/P2xgad-bC

Example Thesis Statements

Many people learn a subject better by seeing multiple examples and how they can be used in writing. Below are examples of different types of thesis statements which could be used for different writing styles. These theses could work for the classroom or the work place.

Expository Theses

Expository writing is the type where the writer explains something. In the classroom, students may need to explain how to use safety goggles in the science lab or practice the skills needed for photographing a landscape. The focus is always on explaining not on persuading or anything else. At work, people might explain how to use new software, how to address a new client or explain a product update.

Examples of Expository Theses

a. I think that everyone has the basic ability to knit and that it can improve people's creativity.

b. When kids today have fewer creative outlets and opportunities for learning a craft, knitting could be taught in schools easily and inexpensively to fill the void.

c. Since knitting improves dexterity and fine motor skills, it should be taught in elementary school.

d. Although some would argue that learning a craft has little value, the skills needed for knitting translate into many areas of life and add to a child's creative experiences.

Analysis

Notice that the above examples include the four styles of thesis statements explained earlier: the basic thesis, the why and what thesis, the data thesis and acknowledging the opposite viewpoint thesis. These thesis statements could be used to write a blog post, answer a question via email, or construct an expository essay. Expository is the most common writing style today. Writers use the expository style throughout essays, journalism, research work, blogging and procedural/how-to writing, so this is a style to know well.

Infographic: Expository Writing

Expository Writing

Expository writing has the purpose of explaining a concept. A writer's job with an expository piece is to take a reader from a point of not knowing very much about the topic to a point of understanding the topic very well.

How does a writer explain?

A writer can explain a topic by including:
*Explanation
*Evidence
*Events
*Statistics
*Quotations
*Conclusions from research
& the inclusion of many other forms of factual information to explain and expand upon the topic.

A good expository essay allows a reader to understand the topic completely.

www.OnDemandInstruction.net

Video: Expository Theses and Support

http://wp.me/P2xgad-bE

Persuasive Theses

Persuasive writing is used nearly as often as expository writing. Persuasive writing is seen in editorials, opinion pieces, persuasive or opinionated blogging, politics, religion, advertising and about anything to do with sales.

In persuasive writing, the writer is trying to convince the reader to agree with a particular viewpoint. Whether the writer wants the reader to buy a product, vote for a candidate, or start a particular diet, the message is persuasive and should be convincing.

The persuasive thesis statement is a convincing one; it is a powerful thesis. The expository thesis statement can be softer because the writer is explaining something, but the persuasive thesis must pack a punch to it. It needs to be strong enough to convince the reader to agree with the writer due to the compelling and irresistible nature of the persuasion and its support.

Examples of Persuasive Theses

a. I believe all children should learn martial arts at school.

b. When children are martial arts trained, their likelihood to bully and to be bullied is significantly lower, so all children should receive martial arts training at school.

c. Since bullying affects 64% of all American students and since martial arts training cuts down on bullying incidents, all children should have free martial arts training through their local schools.

d. Though some may suggest that the expense of ensuring that children grow up in safe communities is too high, training all children in martial arts through the public school system is a small cost resulting in an incredible outcome for communities.

Analysis

Training children in martial arts through public schools is the topic in the above persuasive thesis statement examples. Some people would agree automatically with this idea, whereas others would require a significant amount of convincing to agree. With a persuasive thesis statement that compels the reader to agree, followed by strong support that includes evidence, data and statistics, the reader would be assured the idea is a sound one.

Infographic: Persuasive Writing

On Demand Instruction

Persuasive Writing

Examples of persuasive writing

When you are writing to persuade, you are trying to get people to agree with you on something.

1. Newspaper editorials
2. Reports
3. Speeches
4. Advertisments
5. Reviews

Goal

To take a closer look at your beliefs and the beliefs of others

Use evidence to support your viewpoint, consider views that are against your viewpoint, and write a strong conclusion

Focus your argument on your audience

Identify your audience

Keep in mind the arguments others may have against your viewpoint

Pick an issue that is important to you or that you care about

www.ondemandinstruction.ne

Video: Persuasive Theses and Support

http://wp.me/P2xgad-bG

Narrative Theses

Narrative writing is quite different from expository and persuasive styles. The narrative is a story, and a narrative with a thesis is a narrative essay. In other essay styles, like expository and persuasive, writers tend to be pretty clear on how to structure it, but the narrative is different.

For starters, understand that not every narrative is appropriate for a narrative essay. Many narratives are purely creative and do not connect to a thesis and support. These are not the kind of narratives that would be useful in a narrative essay.

Like the other writing styles, the thesis is the purpose of the narrative essay and the central point of the piece. The thesis is still included in the introduction paragraph, although it may be structured as a precept (moral of the story) and can be presented as foreshadowing.

Examples of Narrative Theses

a. I think last year's camping trip in the mountains taught me to respect nature.

b. When people spend time in nature, especially extended periods of time outdoors, their respect for nature increases.

71

c. Since modern people spend less time outdoors than past generations, our appreciation for the environment has decreased, resulting in a disrespectful attitude towards nature.

d. Although some would say that a week spent in the snowy mountains would be a miserable vacation, last year's camping trip in the mountains left me with a love of the outdoors.

Analysis

In the narrative thesis statement examples above, the thesis statements apply the same structure as the other writing styles, but they are related to a story or narrative. When placed in the introductory paragraph, thesis statements like these provide context, purpose and heightened interest in the narrative. They encourage the reader to engage with the writing.

Infographic: Narrative Writing

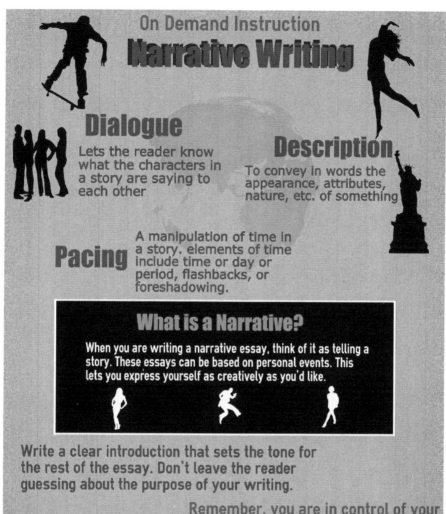

On Demand Instruction

Narrative Writing

Dialogue
Lets the reader know what the characters in a story are saying to each other

Description
To convey in words the appearance, attributes, nature, etc. of something

Pacing
A manipulation of time in a story. elements of time include time or day or period, flashbacks, or foreshadowing.

What is a Narrative?
When you are writing a narrative essay, think of it as telling a story. These essays can be based on personal events. This lets you express yourself as creatively as you'd like.

Write a clear introduction that sets the tone for the rest of the essay. Don't leave the reader guessing about the purpose of your writing.

Remember, you are in control of your essay, so take it where you want it to go! (Just make sure your readers can follow your lead.)

2012 Copyright On Demand Instruction LLC
All Rights Reserved

www.ondemandinstruction.net

Video: Narrative Theses and Support

http://wp.me/P2xgad-bl

Comparison or Contrast Theses

Comparison or contrast writing is probably the most misunderstood of the writing styles. For starters, there are few viable reasons to write a piece that shows comparison and contrast, which would show how two or more things are similar to *and* different from each other. Attempting both comparison and contrast in the same piece typically creates bland, confusing writing. Instead, the writing style works best as comparison *or* contrast, where a writer focuses on only the similarities or the differences of two things. Keeping it simple works best on this style.

For example, a political blogger may cover an upcoming election and point out contrasts between two candidates. While shopping for a new car, a buyer might collect information on the similarities of several vehicles to find which one offers the desired features. A business team may look for the differences in companies to determine which one stands out when reviewing a variety of proposals for a new building project.

Often, students tend to write papers about topics like--how the Audi and the Volkswagen are similar and different—a paper that may create confusion in the end. No one wants to read about how the cars are similar *and* different; readers want to learn about how the Audi is the far superior car or how the Volkswagen is a classic.

The writer should focus on one or the other—comparison or contrast. This narrows the focus of the topics into something that is useful and interesting to the reader and produces a higher-quality piece of writing. It is possible to write a quality piece where the writer compares and contrasts two or more things, but it is unusual because of the inherent difficulties. Stick with comparison *or* contrast wherever possible for better writing.

Examples of Comparison or Contrast Theses

a. I think the two newest Audi sports cars perform too similarly to the decade-old version, making them a disappointment.

b. When considering which of the new Audi sports cars to lease, the higher-end convertible outshines all of the other models.

c. Since this year's new Audis outperform the competition, choosing any of the sports models will result in a satisfying purchase.

d. Although Car Owner Magazine recommended the new Audi sports car, the car's performance decreased from that of the previous models.

Analysis

In the examples above, nowhere were the cars compared *and* contrasted. Instead only a comparison (showing similarities) or a contrast (showing differences) was emphasized in the theses. Theses like these can catch a reader's attention and make the reader want to know why the similarities are so important or why the contrasts stand out. In this case, a strong thesis comes from simplicity.

Infographic: Compare and Contrast: Making Connections

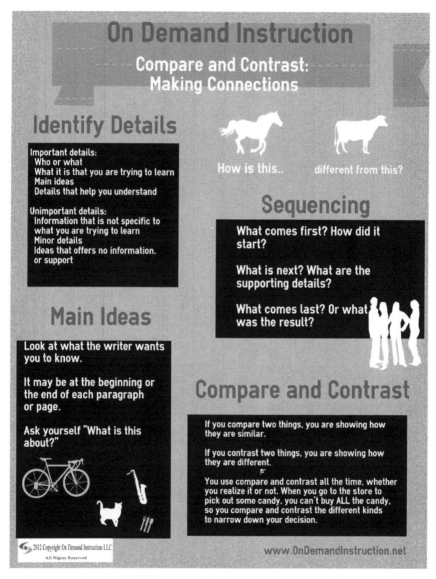

On Demand Instruction
Compare and Contrast: Making Connections

Identify Details

Important details:
Who or what
What it is that you are trying to learn
Main ideas
Details that help you understand

Unimportant details:
Information that is not specific to what you are trying to learn
Minor details
Ideas that offers no information.
or support

How is this.. different from this?

Sequencing

What comes first? How did it start?

What is next? What are the supporting details?

What comes last? Or what was the result?

Main Ideas

Look at what the writer wants you to know.

It may be at the beginning or the end of each paragraph or page.

Ask yourself "What is this about?"

Compare and Contrast

If you compare two things, you are showing how they are similar.

If you contrast two things, you are showing how they are different.

You use compare and contrast all the time, whether you realize it or not. When you go to the store to pick out some candy, you can't buy ALL the candy, so you compare and contrast the different kinds to narrow down your decision.

www.OnDemandInstruction.net

Video: Compare or Contrast Theses and Support

http://wp.me/P2xgad-bK

Research Theses

Research writing utilizes the research process for producing the thesis statement. The research process includes these steps: choosing the topic to research and stating a research question, brainstorming around the topic, researching by reading through a variety of professional materials, organizing the research, and drafting the research into a draft.

Without researching a topic, many writers will start with a thesis statement following their brainstorm process. While brainstorming, writers will collect questions, facts, data and ideas about a topic. After reviewing the compilation of material, a writer will construct the thesis statement based upon the brainstormed content.

Research writing is similar in that a writer will start with a brainstorm, which will contain the results of the research: the data, statistics, survey results and expert quotations. Out of the research comes the thesis statement, because the research guides the thesis statement.

The research process begins with a research question. The writer then researches potential answers to that question; that research becomes the brainstorm. The writer then organizes that research into an outline then drafts the paper upon the outline.

Infographic: What is a Research Paper

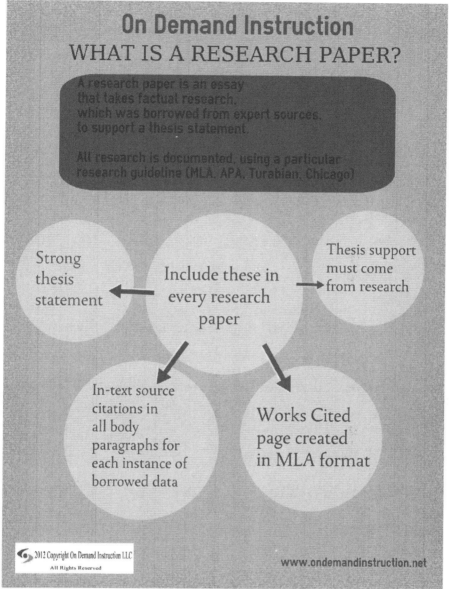

On Demand Instruction

WHAT IS A RESEARCH PAPER?

A research paper is an essay that takes factual research, which was borrowed from expert sources, to support a thesis statement.

All research is documented, using a particular research guideline (MLA, APA, Turabian, Chicago)

Strong thesis statement

Include these in every research paper

Thesis support must come from research

In-text source citations in all body paragraphs for each instance of borrowed data

Works Cited page created in MLA format

www.ondemandinstruction.net

Video: Research Theses and Support

http://wp.me/P2xgad-bM

Examples of Research Theses

a. Research shows that climate change is already happening.

b. When reviewing the data, researchers can observe the effects of climate change today.

c. Since the experts agree that climate change is occurring now, changes to energy policies must be put in place right away.

d. Although some may ignore the available facts, climate change is already occurring throughout the world.

Analysis

The examples above are simple versions of how research theses could be constructed. Keep in mind that a real thesis will always be specific to the research and because of that, may be more specific or narrower in the information included.

Professional Writing

Professional writing falls into any of the writing styles from expository to research. Sometimes in the workplace writers will employ multiple styles at once, so knowing the different styles and how to construct theses and support for each of them can make writing time more productive.

When writing any type of professional piece, consider the audience and what they will need to know.

Also consider the purpose or reason for writing. Once the audience and purpose are established, the writing style and its level of formality should fall into place.

Thesis statements particular to the professional world are no different than those used for other writing.

Video: Professional Theses for the Work Place

http://wp.me/P2xgad-bO

Examples of Professional Theses

a. I think Bell and Trust would do well to reconsider the marketing plan presented by Katy Sherman.

After reviewing the data on last year's profit margins, Bell and Trust should make no changes to investment plans for the coming year.

b. Since profits are up and costs are down for Bell and Trust for the last two years, consideration should be made for expansion in the upcoming year.

c. Although the accounting department holds concerns for the Susan O'Dell's expansion strategy, her plan is clearly well researched and should be considered.

Analysis

The professional writing theses above demonstrate they are no different from the other writing styles. These thesis structures are interchangeable between writing styles as long as audience and purpose are considered.

What

is

Support?

What is Support?

Support includes all of the information that a writer uses to back up a thesis statement. Since the thesis statement is an arguable opinion, the writer must use facts as its foundation.

Some writing is biased like marketing materials, certain editorials, blog posts and political pundit commentary. The biased writer employs an opinionated thesis statement, then uses opinions, conjecture, doubt and assumptions to back up that thesis. This is an ineffective way to write because the outcome produces a less-informed, ill-informed or irritated reader.

For example, if an editorialist suggests that climate change is a hoax then uses biased and opinionated support such as: Aunt Irma's personal opinion, data from a lobbyist for an anti-science group and a conspiracy theorist's blog posting, then the reader is either ignorant as to the actual available data or irritated at having wasted time reading the piece. That is not the effect a writer wants to have on a reader.

All support should be factual in nature, as unbiased as possible and from a quality source.

Infographic: Thesis Support

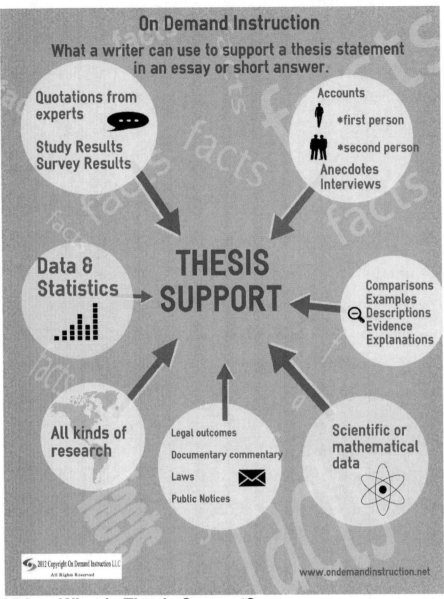

Video: What is Thesis Support?

http://wp.me/P2xgad-bR

Fact and Opinion

Knowing the differences between fact and opinion, and being able to identify those differences quickly, are vital skills for any writer.

Facts are statements or phrases of truth. They can be proven, demonstrated and supported with actual evidence. They are not opinions, not conjecture and not beliefs. Facts can be argued over but ultimately they are indisputable because they can be verified.

Although there are some individuals and groups who choose to ignore, attempt to invalidate, or infuse doubt upon certain facts, facts are still verifiable.

For example, when the tobacco industry executives did not want Americans to stop smoking, they employed marketing experts to spread doubt about the connections between tobacco use and disease. Scientists made the connections between cancer and tobacco, but the industry questioned that data by spreading doubt for their sales purposes. The connections between cancer and tobacco use were true, verifiable facts regardless of the doubt placed upon them.

Writers must be careful of this type of persuasion that tries to manipulate facts and create doubt in the minds of the public. This is just one of the reasons why writers must check the validity of sources before using them as support.

Opinions are the personal or group viewpoints that are not verified as facts. Opinions are undecided or unverified viewpoints.

Everyone has opinions. People's opinions are part of what make them unique individuals and what drive their curiosity and their creativity. But, opinions are not as useful as facts when supporting a thesis in writing.

Bias

Bias is a condition when a person has an opinion about a topic and is not willing to consider contrary ideas. For example, a political pundit may have a bias against people supporting the Labor Party in the United Kingdom and may refuse to consider their ideas.

Bias is found in politics, religion, and business as well as other subjects. When researching a source, determine whether the source holds a particular bias and choose sources that have the least bias. As well, when constructing thesis support, write it bias-free to keep the support factual.

Constructing Support

Covered earlier in this book is the difference between quick writing (when a writer is not able to research before composing the text) and extended writing (when a writer is able to research prior to composing the text). Remember that in quick writing, the thesis is written first and the support follows afterwards. In extended writing, the opposite is true. The research is conducted first and the thesis is a result of the research process.

With this in mind, the writer must consider when to construct the support. Write the thesis statement first and the support afterwards anytime that a response must be created within a time limit and without the benefit of research.

Anytime that the option to research is available, conduct the research first and construct the thesis statement as a result of the research. The research is the support for the thesis statement. Support can look very different depending on the sources and types of research available and applicable to the subject.

Different types of support may include:

- Data
- Statistics

- Quotations
- Examples
- Study results
- Descriptions
- Survey results
- Interviews
- Documentary commentary
- Anecdotes
- Evidence
- Eye witness accounts
- Explanations
- Comparisons
- Legal outcomes

Keep in mind that support is always factual, and information that is factual, comes from a valid source (an expert with verifiable information).

How is Support Used?

Any time that a writer uses a thesis statement to communicate an opinion, then factual support is needed to back up the thesis. The need to support a thesis statement could occur anywhere—in a professional email, in an essay for school or in a blog post. Regardless of the audience and purpose of the writing, the support is always included to prove the thesis.

Short Response Support

The type of support expected in a short response is no different in its content or structure than for a longer piece of writing.

A short response begins with the introduction, which may be a couple of sentences to one paragraph in length. If the introduction is a full paragraph, then that paragraph will include broad, general statements of support for the thesis.

Following the introduction will be the body. In a short answer, this may be a couple of sentences to a couple of paragraphs in length. All of the body will be composed of statements that support the thesis statement. Those support statements will contain data, statistics, explanations, examples and other types of support in an attempt to prove the thesis statement.

Writing Styles

Different Types of Writing Require Different Styles

Persuasive

Persuasive writing is used in situations where the writer wants to convince the reader into agreement.

Examples: advertising, marketing materials, movie trailers, and political speeches or writing.

Expository

Expository writing is where the writer is explaining something to the reader. This may include: informational materials, brochures, websites, and essays. Included in expository writing would be: research papers, health pamphlets, and instructional materials like user's manuals.

Narrative

A narrative is a story. It may be presented as a poem, short story, or dramatic piece. Overall, it is a situation where the writer is telling a story of conflict and its resolution.

Compare/Contrast

Writing that shows how two or more things are either similar or different is comparison/contrast. Typically, a writer will want to stick with either comparison OR contrast not both.

Examples: charts that show product differences, travel brochures that give a list of similar activities in an area, and political materials that show the differences between candidates are all comparison/contrast style.

Research

Research writing is any writing that depends upon researched information from experts to support the thesis statement.

Research can be the most reliable style of writing because the writer is distanced from the topic. The content comes from the researched data, statistics, quotations, and examples from topic experts.

OnDemandInstruction.net

Expository Support

Expository writing is explanatory writing; its purpose is to explain something to the reader. This may be anything from how to make a grilled cheese sandwich to the five reasons that running is a great exercise for middle aged people. Since exposition is explanation, its thesis statement is created to explain a concept to the intended audience and it utilizes factual support to prove the thesis statement.

For example, the writer will use descriptions of every step so that the reader can imitate each of those processes to prepare and cook ratatouille properly when writing an explanation on how to prepare the dish.

While writing an expository article on the best local summer activities for children, the writer may include quotations from last year's participants, descriptions of the activities and detailed data on how to prepare for each of the events.

Since expository writing is explanatory, the writer will choose support that also explains detailed information about the thesis statement. The purpose of the support is always to prove that the thesis is true, which may be presented in different ways depending on the topic.

Infographic: Expository Writing Style Overview

Expository Writing Style

Expository Writing explains or describes

A book that explains the habitats of wild animals is expository writing.

The writer explains what the animals are, what they eat and what their habitats are like. This is expository.

Expository Writing Includes:
* *Book reports
* *Recipes
* *Health and diet books
* *Travel guides
* *Babysitting course lessons
* *Magazines and books about: gardening, cars, space, technology, art history, antique collecting, coins, history, games and animals
* *All essays that explain or describe something

School textbooks are examples of expository writing because they include explanations.

Textbook writers use expository writing to teach a variety of subjects: math, language, social studies and science.

Directions that show how to build something are expository writing. The writer's purpose is to show the reader how to build the project.

Video: Expository Writing Overview

http://wp.me/P2xgad-bT

Persuasive Support

Although persuasive writing has a different purpose, the support employed is similar to that of other writing styles. Persuasive writing will include a strong, persuasive thesis statement that is intended to sway the reader into agreement with the writer on a particular topic.

The persuasive paper's support will all be factual information such as data, statistics, quotations, examples, study results and so forth. One task that the writer needs to consider carefully is how to choose which information will support the thesis and be persuasive to the reader.

When writing persuasive pieces, writers must consider the effect of each element of the writing. If the writer introduces doubt into the overall piece, then the persuasion can be undermined, causing confusion and dissuading the reader from being convinced. This is not the writer's intended outcome.

Instead, persuasive writers should carefully choose support that defends the thesis statement in a definitive manner. When the opportunity arises to address the opposing viewpoint in persuasive writing, do so in a way that demonstrates effectually that the thesis statement is true.

Persuasive writing may include support that demonstrates the barbarity of the death penalty for a piece against the practice. Or it may include statistics on the drop in crime rates to prove that a particular law is effective in stopping crime.

In persuasive writing, the thesis statement is always a strong, arguable opinion that is intended to convince the reader to agree with the writer's viewpoint. Regardless, the support is always factual, verifiable information that is intended to demonstrate the truth in the thesis statement.

Some readers find persuasive writing to be bold or highly opinionated, and in many cases this is true. Since the purpose of the persuasive writer is to convince the reader into agreement, they use all kinds of tactics to solicit the agreement. For example, persuasive writers may appeal to a reader's emotions, logic or ethics, and in fact persuasive writers have been using those particular means of persuasions since Ancient Greece. Appealing to a reader's values can sway a reader into agreement.

Infographic: Persuasive Writing Overview

Persuasive Writing Style

Persuasive writing is that where the writer attempts to persuade or convince the reader into agreement

A writer might draft an opinion editorial for a newspaper on a military topic.

A blog posting about international relations could be a persuasive piece of writing

Writers can create persuasive pieces about any topic, including education and health care

All advertising is persuasive in its purpose and tone. Marketing professionals create persuasive advertisements to convince people to buy their products.

Sports writing is oftentimes persuasive in support of a particular player or team. Sports fans speak and write persuasively when on the subject of their favorite teams.

On Demand Instruction
© Copyright 2013 All Rights Reserved

Video: Persuasive Writing Overview

http://wp.me/P2xgad-bV

Narrative Support

Narrative writing is different from other styles in how it employs support. Since a narrative is a story, it would make little sense to include a list of data, quotations and statistics to support the thesis.

Instead, the narrative will use plot or a series of events to support the thesis statement. The events, the descriptions of characters, the pacing and the revelations in the plot will support the thesis statement in a narrative piece.

For example, when a writer creates a narrative to support a thesis statement like, "Although others complained about the snow, the spring trip to Lake Norden revealed the magic of winter," the story follows the thesis. In this narrative, the rest of the story would support this thesis statement, which completes the connection between thesis and its support.

Narratives can be a little tricky in that the thesis statement is sometimes written last, as it culminates the story but also is the story's purpose. Writers might write the story first, then write the thesis statement, but place the thesis towards the beginning of the narrative so that it is introduced earlier to catch the reader's attention.

Infographic: Narrative Writing Style Overview

Video: Narrative Writing Overview

http://wp.me/P2xgad-bX

Comparison or Contrast Support

The support used for comparison or contrast pieces is the same as the expository support. Since the writer is explaining how two things are either similar or different, then the support will demonstrate through explanation.

For example, if a writing piece is a real estate analysis on the comparisons between two towns then that might include the similarities in the schools, the amenities and the populations. The writer would collect information like crime data, economic statistics and quality of life evidence to demonstrate the similarities between the places.

The writer would include that support in the piece to back up the thesis in an attempt to prove that it is true. This information would be useful to potential home buyers and local businesses.

The same is true when writing a contrast. Choose the support that will best demonstrate how the two contrasted items are different from each other yet supporting the thesis.

For example, a writer might create a brochure that contrasts how a town developed over 20 years but its utilities services were not upgraded. By showing the differences over the 20 years, the writer can attempt to prove the thesis is true and make a strong case for affecting the needed change. Showing the contrasts with evidence, examples and anecdotes would help to accomplish this task.

Infographic: Comparison or Contrast Writing

On Demand Instruction

Comparison OR Contrast Writing

Look at two topics or subjects and discuss how they are similar OR different.

Introduction

Open with an anecdote, generalization, or quotation and write a lead into the thesis statement.

Topic 1

Cover the first topic that you're going to compare OR contrast in great detail.

Topic 2

This is the where you go into Topic 2 in great detail. Include: facts, evidence, details, in-text citations, and research

Topics 1 & 2 together

Now is the time to bring your two topics together, contrasting the two subjects and showing their similarities OR differences. This could be several paragraphs.

Conclusion

Like the introduction, this should be a generalization of your thesis statement. Restate your thesis and show how you've proven it with your major points.

www.OnDemandInstruction.net

Video: Comparison or Contrast Writing Overview

http://wp.me/P2xgad-bZ

Research Support

Anytime that a writer is conducting research prior to writing the thesis statement, the connection between the support and thesis is a natural one.

When a writer follows the writing process, then the typical steps are: brainstorming and researching around the research question, organizing the results into an outline, composing the thesis statement and creating the paper's draft which includes both the thesis and the support.

The support is composed on the sum of the research. That may include any of the different types of support listed previously: data, statistics, quotations, examples, study results, descriptions and so on.

One big difference when composing research writing is that the research will be cited using a style guide (like MLA, APA, AP, Turabian, etc.). The writer cites the research in both the body paragraphs with in-text citations and in a Bibliography or Works Cited page at the end. The support in research writing is factual, unbiased and from quality sources wherever possible. The writer includes the support in an attempt to prove that the thesis statement is

true. By employing research as support, the writer is
engaging the expertise of professionals, academics and
experts to assist in supporting the thesis statement. This
method is a powerful means of supporting a thesis
statement.

Anytime that research is being conducted, writers
need to ensure the research sources are properly
documented. For instance, when writing an article that
includes a quotation from another writer, be sure to give
credit by declaring clearly the writer's name and the source.
One way to do this is to preface the quotation by stating the
cited information:

"In the article 'One Flew Over New York' from the
New Year Magazine, writer Margaret Trammel stated,
"Although so many millions of immigrants have moved into
and out of New York's boroughs during the city's four
century tenure as landing spot, New York is best known as
the cultural melting pot meets mixed salad. It is the city
where cultural innovation continues to grow."

By making it very clear where your researched
information comes from, writers add a layer of validity and
quality to their writing. Readers are able to recognize the
source of the research and make decisions about the
writer's content off of that.

Infographic: Research Writing Style Overview

Research Writing Style

Research writers conduct research before composing their writing

Research Writing Steps
1. Pose a research question
2. Conduct the research
3. Organize the research
4. Write the first draft

Researchers always report on the results of the research not on their opinions, popular views or other things.

Examples of research writing:

Survey results
Documentaries
Investigations
Incident reports
Literary papers
Scientific research
Social science books

Research writing also includes a Works Cited or Bibliography page where research sources are listed

Video: Research Writing Overview

http://wp.me/P2xgad-c1

Organize

the

Writing

Organize the Writing

Learning what a thesis statement is and how to support it is a great start. With that knowledge, writers can say what they need to and get their points across intelligently. But, what about the ways those points are made? Is there anything else to the process than just stating a viewpoint and supporting it? There is—organization.

Information that is organized tends to appeal to readers. Most readers want to understand the material quickly rather than have to work through the text.

Sometimes readers skim a text in search of specific information. Perhaps a reader is looking for the thesis statement. Or maybe the reader is looking for statistics or data that support the thesis.

A certain type of organization must be in place for the reader to be satisfied while skimming through a text. This is because readers are used to a straightforward organizational style for most writing.

The most basic and most common elements of organization are: introduction, body and conclusion. Regardless of the piece of writing, these three elements are necessary. Letters, research papers, essays, blog posts and memos all need introduction, body and conclusion.

Writers who want to connect with an audience easily stick to these basic elements. This makes planning a piece of writing easier on the writer and makes reading comprehension easier on the reader.

Why Organize?

The best argument in the world will fall flat if it is hidden in a disorganized mess of an essay. Not only it is vitally important to have something of value to communicate, but it is necessary to organize that information in an appealing format for the reader.

When a reader opens a piece of writing, that person holds certain expectations of the writer. For example, when a citizen sends a letter to a state representative asking for information on an issue, the letter needs to be in a letter format. This format will allow the reader to understand the message more easily.

Every writer shares the goal of communicating easily with the reader. When a reader shakes the head or shrugs the shoulders because an essay is too confusing or too disorganized, that writer is in trouble.

The disorganized writer sends the wrong message to readers. For example, the writer who leaves the thesis statement until the end of the essay confuses the audience through the whole paper. The blogger who rambles through a series of examples but states no viewpoint will lose followers. Also, the advertiser who never tells the audience to buy the particular product might lose sales rather than make them.

Readers judge writers by their viewpoint, content, style, organization and overall presentation. Disorganized writers tend to be judged poorly. This is the case even when their viewpoints and support are the very best.

To make the best impression on readers and communicate viewpoints with clarity, use a logical organization in all writing.

The best way to produce organized writing is to be organized throughout the writing process. The traditional writing process includes these steps:

- Brainstorming
- Organizing
- Drafting
- Editing and Revising
- Final Drafting (or Preparing for Presentation or Publication)

Readers who happen across disorganized writing will perceive that the writer followed muddled process while creating the writing. Disordered writing tends to turn off readers, and that bad news for writers. Closely following the writing process, especially the first two steps of brainstorming and organizing, help writers produce organized writing.

Infographic: Why Organize Your Writing?

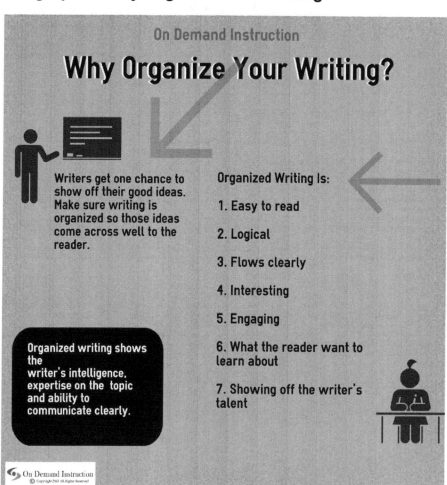

Introduction Paragraphs

Every piece of writing begins with some kind of an introduction. Everything from a single paragraph to a novel-length book contains an introduction of sorts. The introduction could be as brief as a single sentence or it could be several pages long. The length all depends on what is needed for the piece of writing.

If the piece of writing is just a paragraph long, then a single sentence should suffice as an introduction. That sentence will be the first sentence in the paragraph and will introduce the reader to the topic and purpose of the writing. That first sentence could be either a hook statement or the thesis statement; either work well in that position.

Say that a paragraph response is needed to answer the prompt: What meal do most teenagers like best? **Possible single-sentence introductions could include:**

- If you have a teenager in your home, then you are always on the lookout for healthy, hearty meals.
- 80% of teenagers say they want meals that fill them up and can be eaten on the run.

- Did you know that teenagers want to eat healthy meals but feel like they lack options?

Any of these sentences could work for a one-sentence introduction to one-paragraph long response. That introduction serves two purposes: catching the reader's attention and letting the reader know what the piece is about. Readers want to know from the very beginning what a piece is about. They want to know what the viewpoint is so that they can choose whether to engage or not with the piece. A strong introduction encourages the reader.

In a one-paragraph response, the introduction is just a sentence long. That is easy enough to construct. But what about a longer piece? In a longer piece of writing, the introduction should be 5-25% of the total length of the piece.

So, for a traditional-length book, the introduction might be an entire chapter long. This could be anywhere from 5 to 25 pages just depending on the book's topic, its overall length and how much information the writer needs to divulge before the book's main content begins.

Balance needs to be struck between the length of the introduction and the piece it introduces. A one-sentence introduction for a full-length book would be completely unsatisfying. And a one paragraph introduction for a two paragraph response would be overwhelming. Making that connection between how much to share with the reader before sharing the meat of the content is an important balance to strike.

The most typical piece of writing is an essay. The essay is usually no shorter than four or five paragraphs in length. In this situation, the introduction should be the first paragraph. The essay's introduction is going to take up anywhere from 5-25% of the total length of the piece. For a four-paragraph essay, one paragraph takes up a quarter of the total length. A ten-page or twenty-paragraph essay with a one-paragraph introduction means that the introduction takes less space but still needs to introduce the topic.

The traditional essay format is used everywhere and not just for essays. This includes: introduction, body and conclusion. Blog postings, editorials, emails, letters and other types of writing all use the basic essay format. This makes the essay format and its purpose incredibly important to understand.

For an essay, the introduction should catch the reader's attention, tell the reader what the topic is, give the reader the thesis statement and give some general support statement for the thesis.

Infographic: Introduction Paragraphs

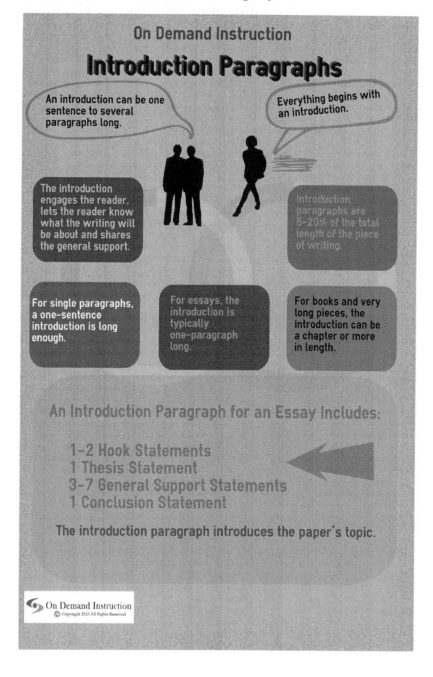

Start an introduction by catching the reader's attention. **There are several different ways to do this:**

- Rhetorical question
- Interesting statistic
- Brief story
- Quotation
- Current event comparison

These five methods work well to catch a reader's attention. Any writer can use one or two of these devices at the beginning of an essay's introduction paragraph.

Rhetorical Question

The rhetorical question is one the writer does not intend to be answered. Instead, it is a question that gets the reader thinking about the essay's topic. The question should be interesting and should engage the reader right away.

Examples of rhetorical questions:

- Do you realize that in 2015 more refugees were made homeless and stateless than in any year since 1945?
- Does a healthy diet really require eight glasses of water per day?
- Is global warming actually a conspiracy by scientists?

None of these questions should be answered by the reader even though the writer asks them. Instead, they serve the purpose of engaging the reader to the essay and getting the reader excited to continue reading. Catching a reader's attention can be a challenge, especially in today's world of competing electronic distractions. So, a strong rhetorical question can go a long way to grabbing the reader at the beginning.

Introduction paragraphs should start off with a hook or catch statement. A "hook" or "catch" are two terms for the same thing—phrases or sentences that grab the reader's attention. Since writers are competing with ever-increasing distractions for people's attention. To produce interesting writing, consider grabbing the reader's attention at the very beginning of each piece of writing with a hook or catch statement.

Infographic: Rhetorical Questions in Introduction Paragraphs

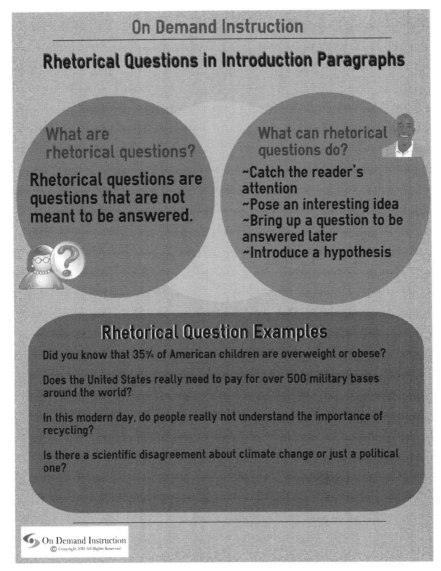

Video: Rhetorical Questions as Hook Statements

http://wp.me/P2xgad-dN

Interesting Statistic

Interesting statistics also do well to grab the reader at the very beginning of the essay. Today, people are interested in knowing the data, math and science behind the topic. They want to know the statistics so that they can make their own decisions. Starting with a statistic is a great way to catch the reader's attention from the very beginning of the essay. **Examples of interesting statistics:**

- In the United States 19.6% of high school students reported being bullied in the last year and 64% who were bullied did not report it.

- Today, about 600,000 hysterectomies are performed each year resulting in 30% of all women over 40 having undergone the procedure.

- Over half of the world's population live on less than $2.50 per day and experience the harsh effects of poverty.

These interesting statistics might not reveal to the reader what the thesis statement is, but they do reveal what the essay's topic is. They should engage the reader by offering an interesting statistic at the very beginning of the essay to grab the reader's attention. Often, statistics cause the reader to become curious about the topic and want to know more details on it. That is the kind of engagement the writer wants.

Infographic: Interesting Statistics in Introduction Paragraphs

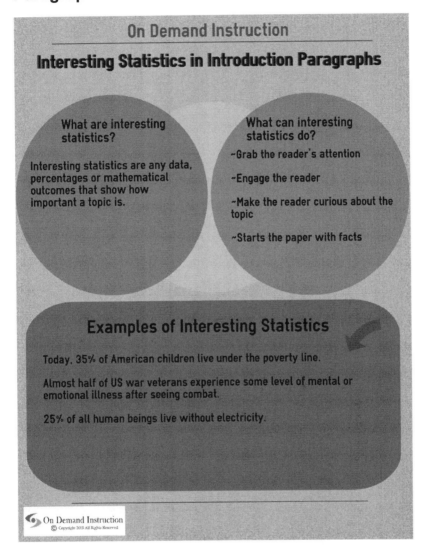

On Demand Instruction

Interesting Statistics in Introduction Paragraphs

What are interesting statistics?

Interesting statistics are any data, percentages or mathematical outcomes that show how important a topic is.

What can interesting statistics do?

~Grab the reader's attention

~Engage the reader

~Make the reader curious about the topic

~Starts the paper with facts

Examples of Interesting Statistics

Today, 35% of American children live under the poverty line.

Almost half of US war veterans experience some level of mental or emotional illness after seeing combat.

25% of all human beings live without electricity.

On Demand Instruction
© Copyright 2015 All Rights Reserved

Video: Interesting Statistics as a Hook Statement

http://wp.me/P2xgad-dQ

Brief Story

A brief story is another great way to engage the reader at the beginning of an essay. Most people love a good story, even one that lasts just a couple of sentences. Humans are naturally drawn to narratives and tend to engage quickly with stories. The brief story can be a little more challenging to compose but can have a positive effect on the essay.

Examples of brief stories:

- The six-year old boy named Falcon supposedly floated into the sky after his hot air balloon detached from its mooring. Really, he slept the afternoon in the family's attic. Although the guilty parents of the balloon boy are moving on with their lives, they demonstrate the current obsession with fame and creating fake lives for reality TV.

- Teddy Bear and I went everywhere until the day he was lost. After three years he was returned in tattered condition; I took one look at him, called him a "runaway" and left him on the sidewalk.

- I asked Santa for a new bike year after year to no avail. Finally, I bought my own and realized Santa would never come through for me.

These stories are only a sentence or two long, but they give a vision of what the whole story could be about. These stories hold poignant tales of sadness, loss and change.

They create an excellent hook to catch the reader's attention at the very beginning of the essay and give the reader a window into the topic to be covered.

Infographic: Brief Story in Introduction Paragraphs

On Demand Instruction

Brief Story in Introduction Paragraphs

What are brief stories?

Brief stories are very short narratives used in an introduction paragraph.

What can a brief story do?

~Engage the reader right away

~Show how something works or is true

~Make a point by giving an example

~Add humor or interest to writing

Examples of Brief Stories

A 14 year old boy was arrested and charged with assault after kissing a classmate. The incident cost his parents $3200 to keep him out of jail, making it an incredibly expensive prank gone wrong.

Today Enrique a 16-year old teenager from Alabama continues his long, lonely journey. He has been left in solitary confinement for two years for stealing a television while in middle school and lives alone in a solitary cell.

She placed one foot in front of the other. Over and over thousands of times a day. During a five-month trek, Caroline Jackson walked from Southern California to Washington State on the Pacific Coast Trail.

Video: Brief Story as a Hook Statement

http://wp.me/P2xgad-dT

Quotation

Using a quotation from a famous person or subject matter expert is the most common style of hook statement. By starting an essay with a quote from someone important, the writer connects to that person. By connecting to a famous or valuable expert, the writer suggests the topic that is highly important. Quotations are a great way to connect the reader to the topic and engage the reader to keep reading from the beginning.

Examples of quotations:

- "You don't learn from successes; you don't learn from awards; you don't learn from celebrity; you only learn from wounds and scars and mistakes and failures. And that's the truth." Jane Fonda
- Tyra Banks once said, "If I tried to start modeling right now, I wouldn't be a supermodel because it's all about celebrity."
- An ancient Chinese proverb goes like this, "The best time to plant a tree was 20 years ago. The next best time is today."

These quotations get the reader thinking about the essay's topic right away. If the essay is about learning life lessons, modeling or the environment, the reader catches onto that immediately. By choosing a well-phrased quotation, the writer connects to someone more expert than oneself. This allows the reader to connect to the piece of writing and to its topic right away. The writer may want to use a single quotation at the beginning of the introduction then follow up with a single-sentence explanation before launching into the rest of the introduction paragraph. Sometimes this can be useful to guide the reader in the specific direction the writer intends.

Infographic: Quotations in Introduction Paragraphs

On Demand Instruction
Quotations in Introduction Paragraphs

What are quotations?

Quotations are words taken from a piece of writing, speech, show or some other format. They are exact, word-for-word statements of the original speech.

What can quotations do?

~Interest the reader in the writing

~Connect the writer or the writing to a famous person, group or expert

~Point out a connection between the writing and another topic

Examples of Quotations

"Example is leadership." Albert Schweitzer

"Ask not what your country can do for you but what you can do for your country." President John F. Kennedy

"Adventure is worthwhile in itself." Amelia Earhart

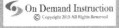
Video: Quotations as Hook Statements

http://wp.me/P2xgad-dW

Current Event

The current event is another way to hook the reader at the beginning of the essay. In today's world of prolific media outlets, most people are up to date on current events, even if they have just the basic information. Making a connection to a current event, either comparison or contrast, can connect the essay to something tangible for the reader. Many readers view current events as highly valuable, so making that association can heighten the sense of importance in the essay.

Examples of current events:

- Perhaps if scientists can evaluate the newest studies, they can diagnose the reason that 18% of children suffer from severe food allergies.

- The current decision to reference people as migrants, asylum-seekers or refugees can hold dramatic consequences on how they are viewed by the public and the kind of assistance they receive.

- Significant confusion still exists over people's individual rights to free speech and their duties to perform job responsibilities while public employees.

These current events connect the essay's topic to what is happening in the world today. By connecting current events to the essay's topic, the writer makes it easy for the reader to gain a sense of the essay's importance. This hook pulls

the reader into the essay and encourages the reader to
continue through the paper and learn about the
information included.

Infographic: Current Events in Introduction Paragraphs

On Demand Instruction

Current Events in Introduction Paragraphs

What are current events?

Current events are incidents happening on a local, national or international level. People who keep up with the news typically know the current events.

What can current events do?

~Connect the essay's topic to a current event

~Point out the importance of the topic

~Emphasize some commentary about people, groups or events

Examples of Current Events

With the passage of marijuana legalization laws in Colorado and Washington, surrounding states are battling new issues as never before.

Shocking the tennis world, Flavia Pennetta beat Serena Williams at age 33 and won the US Open.

The annual Lafayette Peach Festival kicks off today, which brings in 20,000 people across the state to sample the region's sweetest peaches.

Video: Current Events as Hook Statements

http://wp.me/P2xgad-dZ

The essay is the most common writing format. It is copied into blogs, editorials, letters and other writing purposes. Because of this, the writer can apply this format to many uses and become more proficient over time with essay writing.

The hook statement is just the beginning of the introduction paragraph. Once the hook is in place, the writer has two choices: state the thesis next or state the general support next. The two ways of structuring an introduction paragraph are listed below.

Option 1: State the thesis early in the introduction paragraph.

1. One or two hook statements
2. Thesis statement
3. Three to seven general support statements
4. Conclusion statement

Option 2: State the thesis later on in the introduction paragraph.

1. One or two hook statements
2. Three to seven general support statements
3. Thesis statement
4. Conclusion statement

In the first option, the writer expresses the thesis statement following the hook statements. This lets the reader know right away what the essay's topic is and what viewpoint the writer is defending in this essay.

In the second option, the writer communicates the general support before the thesis statement. This allows the writer to build up to the revelation of the thesis statement. The writer creates a sense of support and positive outcome by doing this.

Both of these structures of introductory paragraphs work well and both could be used in a wide variety of writing and essay styles. The important factor is that the basic purposes of the introduction have been met: engaging the reader, informing the reader of the essay's topic and stating the thesis statement. The writer must achieve those purposes in the introduction.

Infographic: Introduction Paragraphs

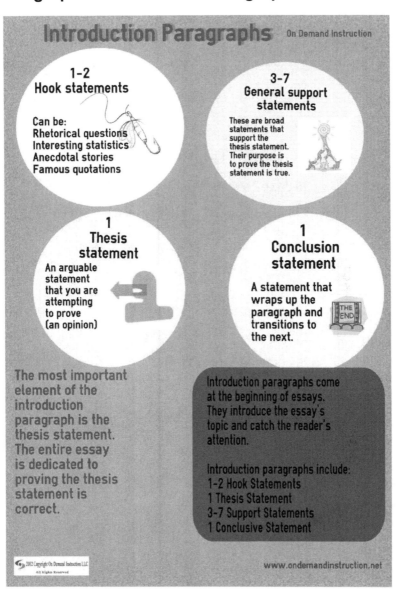

Introduction Paragraphs
On Demand Instruction

1-2 Hook statements

Can be:
Rhetorical questions
Interesting statistics
Anecdotal stories
Famous quotations

3-7 General support statements

These are broad statements that support the thesis statement. Their purpose is to prove the thesis statement is true.

1 Thesis statement

An arguable statement that you are attempting to prove (an opinion)

1 Conclusion statement

A statement that wraps up the paragraph and transitions to the next.

THE END

The most important element of the introduction paragraph is the thesis statement. The entire essay is dedicated to proving the thesis statement is correct.

Introduction paragraphs come at the beginning of essays. They introduce the essay's topic and catch the reader's attention.

Introduction paragraphs include:
1-2 Hook Statements
1 Thesis Statement
3-7 Support Statements
1 Conclusive Statement

www.ondemandinstruction.net

Video: Introduction Paragraphs

http://wp.me/P2xgad-e2

Body Paragraphs

In an essay, the body is the main portion of the writing. It can be anywhere from two to two dozen paragraphs long. The body paragraphs all have the same function which is to support the thesis statement. How do they do this?

The body paragraphs include data, statistics, quotations, examples, anecdotes, details, expert testimony, evidence, and the results from research, surveys and studies. A writer can use any of these to support the thesis statement, which is indicated in the introduction paragraph.

The body paragraphs can vary in length but are typically not longer than two-thirds of a page. Sometimes they can be as short as a single sentence for blogs or articles, but in essays, body paragraphs are generally longer than four sentences.

Body paragraphs start with an introduction sentence. This sentence has two purposes—to transition from the previous paragraph and to introduce the topic covered in that paragraph. After the introduction sentence, the writer includes support sentences and detail sentences. Then the writer ends the body paragraph with a conclusion sentence.

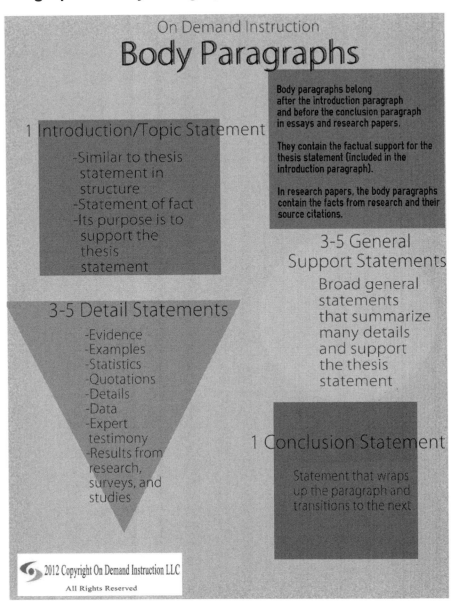

On Demand Instruction

Body Paragraphs

Body paragraphs belong after the introduction paragraph and before the conclusion paragraph in essays and research papers.

They contain the factual support for the thesis statement (included in the introduction paragraph).

In research papers, the body paragraphs contain the facts from research and their source citations.

1 Introduction/Topic Statement
- Similar to thesis statement in structure
- Statement of fact
- Its purpose is to support the thesis statement

3-5 General Support Statements
Broad general statements that summarize many details and support the thesis statement

3-5 Detail Statements
- Evidence
- Examples
- Statistics
- Quotations
- Details
- Data
- Expert testimony
- Results from research, surveys, and studies

1 Conclusion Statement
Statement that wraps up the paragraph and transitions to the next

Block Format Paragraphs

There are a couple of different ways to structure body paragraphs. One of those is to use a block method, which allows the writer to focus each paragraph on one topic.

In the block method, the writer centers each paragraph on one topic or one point and exhausts all of the details about that point before moving on. For example, if an essay is about how to make salsa, the writer may spend an entire paragraph explaining how to prepare the tomatoes before moving on to the spices. That body paragraph is all about the one topic—tomato preparation.

In an essay or other piece of writing, each body paragraph concentrates on just one point. This creates a logical and straightforward flow for the reader to keep up with the points the writer states throughout the piece.

The block method works particularly well for covering complicated subjects. When each topic requires a more in-depth explanation for the reader to understand, breaking up those larger topics into individual points can make the presentation smoother.

Another good use for the block method is the comparison or contrast essay. When using the block method, the writer would focus on just one point for each body paragraph. So, in a comparison essay, focus on how the two objects are similar on one topic for that paragraph.

When used with the comparison or contrast essay, the writer uses the block method to direct the reader fluidly through the sequence of the comparisons.

As well, the block paragraph could be used in a cause and effect piece. When showing the progression of events, the writer could follow a chronological, thematic or chain of events organization. The block format allows the writer to focus each paragraph on one topic. If the writer is creating a cause and effect piece on how a mud slide occurs after a rain, then the first body paragraph could be about the rain. The second body paragraph could be about the soil changes caused by the rain. The third paragraph could be about the loosening of soil which causes the mudslide. The effects of each of these topics would be covered either in a fourth body paragraph or in the conclusion paragraph. By organizing the paragraphs block style, the writer creates logically-organized content.

Using the block method for creating body paragraphs makes organized, easy-to-understand paragraphs that are focused on one topic each. Writers can connect the paragraphs with transition words or phrases that link the essay's topics together. By doing this, the writer creates an easy-to-understand essay.

Point by Point Format Paragraphs

Another way to format a body paragraph is using the point by point format. In this method, the writer covers the details of one idea, theme or subtopic in each paragraph before moving on.

Writers use the point by point method to focus on themes or ideas that cross more than one topic. This means that writers cover multiple topics in each body paragraph. For example, in an expository essay on American writers, one body paragraph might cover male writers and include Thoreau, Hemingway and Hughes. The second body paragraph might cover female writers and cover Walker, Angelou and Alcott. Each paragraph includes multiple topics but follows one general idea or theme.

In a cause and effect piece, the writer could use the point by point format to organize all of the body paragraphs. The first body paragraph could cover the first topic of rain, its causes and its effects. The second paragraph could cover the second topic of soil changes, its causes and its effects. The third paragraph could cover the third topic of the mudslide, its causes and its effects. Since the causes and effects were covered in the body paragraphs, the writer would not need to cover the effects in a separate paragraph.

The point by point method works well to organize the overall topics by themes. This allows the reader to understand the broader topics throughout the paper. It also removes the need to summarize throughout the piece. Many writers are drawn to this organizational format.

Conclusion Paragraphs

Every piece of writing should end in some kind of conclusion, even if that conclusion is just a single sentence long. The conclusion acts as the final opportunity to leave the reader with a memory of the writing. Every piece of writing should end powerfully, whether a one paragraph email or a full-length novel.

In a short piece of writing, a single sentence can wrap up the whole piece. This sentence operates as the conclusion and is the last sentence of the piece. The writer should focus on a brief summary or rewording of the thesis in the one-sentence conclusion.

In a longer piece, the conclusion is typically one paragraph long. It is usually organized in a similar manner to the introduction paragraph, except shorter. The conclusion should begin with a general summary statement as the first sentence. Then it should include three to seven support statements, each of which supports the thesis. And the conclusion wraps up the whole piece by restating the thesis.

A book-length piece may need several paragraphs or even a whole chapter to conclude the piece. The conclusion's purpose is the same—summarize the most valuable information for the reader. Leave the reader with a strong sense of what the piece is about. The conclusion is the very last opportunity to communicate with the author, so make a strong impression.

Infographic: Conclusion Paragraphs

On Demand Instruction

Conclusion Paragraphs

Conclusion Paragraphs

Conclusion paragraphs are used in all essays and research papers. Their purpose is to wrap up the paper. They include:
*An introduction sentence
*3-7 general support statements
*A conclusive statement

General support statements

Broad general statements that summarize and synthesize many details, all of which support the thesis statement.

Start with an introduction/topic sentence

Similar to a thesis statement in construction

Statement of fact

Its purpose is to support the thesis statement

Conclusion statement

Statement that wraps up the paper and focuses on the thesis statement.

Restate the thesis.

Finish with a strong conclusion statement that encourages the reader to agree with your thesis.

Keeping the Reader's Attention

While working on any piece, writers need to consider how to present the thesis statement, give the support and keep the reader interested throughout the piece. Even if the piece is a few sentences long, the reader can feel lost or bored quickly.

A couple of tools help writers to keep the reader's attention. One is to use transition words or phrases. These serve to keep the flow of the piece moving forward.

Here are several types of transitions:

- Numeric: one, two, three
- Chronological: first, second, third
- Hierarchal: best, better, good
- Time Related: after, during, meanwhile
- Comparisons: in the same way, similarly, like
- Emphasis: to repeat, again, moreover
- Conclusion or Summary: as a result, therefore, to sum up
- Clarification: in other words, for instance, put another way

Writers can include transition words at the beginning of paragraphs or mixed within them. Both work well. Transition words improve the writing's flow, which makes it more appealing.

Another way to keep the reader's attention is to take the reader into consideration. When writing, try to use vocabulary that is on the level the reader wants. For example, when writing a blog posting to high school students, use language appropriate to teenagers. When writing an academic paper, use academic language specific to the piece. Readers do not typically enjoy writing that is too high or too low for their reading levels.

Finally, another way to keep the reader's attention is to follow the standard writing expectations for that genre. Be sure to edit and correct all errors before sharing the piece. Errors distract readers from the messages in the writing. Ensure that the information included is accurate and up to date. Also, anytime that research is conducted, then properly cite the sources used. Finally, try to be yourself when writing. The message you bring is more interesting when written with your voice.

Infographic: Keeping the Reader's Attention

Keeping the Reader's Attention

> Use vocabulary appropriate to the audience.

The writer wants the reader to keep going, keep reading the piece. It is important not to lose the reader along the way. Keep the reader interested by making the writing interesting.

Transitions Show Change

- Numeric: one, two, three
- Chronological: first, second, third
- Hierarchal: best, better, good
- Time Related: after, during, meanwhile
- Comparisons: in the same way, similarly, like
- Emphasis: to repeat, again, moreover
- Conclusion or Summary: as a result, therefore, to sum up
- Clarification: in other words, for instance, put another way

Meet the reader's expectations.

If the reader expects a well-written piece, make sure to create a well-written piece.

Writing Examples

Thesis and Support

Writing Examples-Thesis and Support

Most people understand best by looking over examples when learning something new. We included several examples below of full length pieces of writing followed by explanations on what we included and why. Hopefully these examples show how thesis statements can be used and supported in completed pieces of writing. Any of these pieces could be used as essays, blog posts, letters, and editorials or for professional purposes.

The examples below include expository, persuasive, comparison or contrast, research and narrative writing styles. The writing levels vary from a seventh grade to adult reading level to demonstrate how to appeal to a variety of audiences. Since essays must take a strong stance on current issues, the following essays are purposely opinionated; they are intended to instruct not to offend. If the topic causes offense, know that it is using a strong thesis and essay format, which is the purpose of theses.

Example Expository Blog Post

Write an expository blog post highlighting why your town is a great place to live.

Some people suggest that small towns have little to offer culturally for professional families. Since some small towns are limited in multiculturalism, art galleries, science museums and small business support, they tend to be less appealing to a young professional than cities. Although some small towns may be less culturally diverse and rich in opportunity, Longmont, CO is one of the most attractive small towns in America for professional families. Longmont's long-standing support for small businesses is unparalleled in the country. Its cultural facilities include art, science and sports centers. Overall, Longmont is a fantastic place to live for any professional.

One of the primary reasons for Longmont's attraction is its location. At the north-eastern edge of Boulder, County, Longmont boasts some of the most beautiful scenery in the country. Longmont residents wake up to a gorgeous view of Longs Peak; the mountain gives Longmont residents a breathtaking backdrop for the town named for it. The town boasts dozens of fishing ponds, hiking trails, biking paths, mountain communities and small farms within just a few miles. Longmont is close to everything.

As well, Longmont is not a homogenous small town. It boasts a multicultural community including every socio-economic class with nearly every ethnic, political and religious group represented. Here, folks enjoy making friends with a wide variety of people while engaged in the town's inclusive activities. The Farmer's Market, Longmont Museum and multiple recreation centers facilitate free or inexpensive cultural experiences.

Too, Longmont is home to a thriving small business culture. Artists, brewers, farmers and creatives find Longmont a welcome and supporting community. The area advocates buying local products, supporting artists as well as several business associations working to supporting small businesses. Overall, Longmont is a great town to start or run a small business.

In conclusion, Longmont cannot be beat as a small town for young professional families. Its cultural amenities, proximity to outdoor activities and positive environment make it an ideal home.

Expository Blog Post Analysis

In this blog posting, we see a few paragraphs explaining how Longmont, CO is a great place for young professional families. The audience has been clearly identified—young professionals. The tone is expository because the writer explains throughout the piece the benefits of living in this town. The purpose is to explain.

The thesis statement is: Although some small towns may be less culturally diverse and rich in opportunity, Longmont, CO is one of the most attractive small towns in America for professional families. The writer is acknowledging that some people might have the viewpoint that small towns lack what young professionals seek in a home. Those assumptions are refuted by explaining all that Longmont has to offer.

The support that Longmont is a great home includes: natural beauty, cultural diversity, proximity to outdoor activities and support for small businesses. The writer suggests that these are the appealing factors that young professionals look for in a small town.

Other support that the writer could have included might include: schools, education levels, crime statistics, weather, green infrastructure and other amenities. This blog post could be expanded into a longer piece by looking into these other topics. Another way to expand this piece would be by including detailed descriptions of particular locations around town or by interviewing residents for quotes that would explain the benefits of the Longmont lifestyle. This piece could be used as a blog post, a brochure or an essay.

Example Persuasive Editorial

Persuade a reader to agree with your viewpoint on state testing of public school students.

Over the past two decades, the United States has followed a singular policy to vilify American public schools, label those with lower socio-economic groups as failing and depend heavily on standardized tests. These tests, as has been demonstrated for decades, function as poor determiners of instructional quality, student ability and school viability. Rather than serving the public school student, the tests fail to provide quality data on student outcomes. Not only are the tests unable to give quality data, their administration and data collection methods are illogically designed. Overall, standardized tests function better as a means for undermining quality education than improving it.

As has been revealed since the 1970s, American students have consistently performed poorly on standardized tests. Yet, Americans are the very people who have demonstrated leadership in innovation, creativity and entrepreneurship internationally. Americans are always at the forefront of new businesses and international development. As well, the test scores have changed little overall in 40 years of American education. The scores that the X-generation earned are similar to the scores the millennials earned.

The testing system does not hold up to its own data analysis let alone any other. For example, since 2002, a year after President Bush signed No Child Left Behind into law, American test scores have actually dropped. This alone demonstrates the futility of millions of dollars spent testing and teaching to the tests. Too, there are no studies that demonstrate that standardized testing improves education. If there are research studies that show testing as an improvement in education, perhaps the millions spent each year could be justified, but this is not the case.

Unfortunately, legislatures decided to get behind the trend of judging teachers, students and schools according to standardized tests. It is too bad they did not do their homework to find out if the tests worked or would provide the intended outcomes before implementing these practices into laws. It is time to end the cycle of testing and apply workable methods to improve education.

Persuasive Writing Analysis

In this editorial, we see a very different piece of writing than the previous one. In this piece, the writer does not identify the audience, but by looking at the newspaper that published this piece, the audience might be implied. The tone is determined and confident, and the purpose is to persuade.

The thesis statement is: These tests, as has been demonstrated for decades, function as poor determiners of instructional quality, student ability and school viability. The writer points out that standardized testing has not solved the problems in American education. The writer points out both specific situations as well as data to back up this thesis.

The support includes comparing contemporary American education to that of 40 years ago. The writer uses statistics and data to support the thesis. Also, the writer points out the starting point of the problem, the 2001 law No Child Left Behind, and the people responsible for it, legislatures.

Other support that the writer could have brought up might include: quotations from educational leaders and statistics showing more supporting data. This editorial would come across as strong since the writer takes a robust, persuasive stance on the issue. It could also be used as an essay, testimonial or letter to a legislature.

Example Narrative Story

Write a personal narrative about an important life lesson.

Although I find it incredibly hard to follow through on, allowing my child to fail creates the best learning opportunities. In today's world, many parents succumb to a helicopter or hyper-protective parenting practice, which does not prepare children for an independent, responsible adulthood. The parents' reasons are that their children are more successful with parent assistance and children's time is wasted when troubleshooting problems which parents can fix quickly. When teaching my young son about money management, I realized how important that allowing him to fail really is.

My son Max earns $5 per week after completing his chore chart. This chore chart lists out the activities he is expected to complete each day. Doing well at them earns him a star and doing poorly earns him an X. A chart full of stars is worth $5 a week, each X can lose Max $1, and a additional good deed can earn him an extra star or $1.

During the first week of summer, Max was particularly lazy on Tuesday and earned two Xs, one for not cleaning his toys out of the living room and one for not putting away his dishes after dinner. He scored an extra star on Wednesday for helping dig the garden without being asked, but then lost a star on Thursday for failing to brush his hair and teeth before leaving the house. On Friday, he lost another star for refusing to turn off the TV after three warnings. By Saturday morning, Max's pay day included only $2.

On our typical Saturday ritual, we headed to the farmer's market to pick up our food for the week.

"Mama, where can I spend my money?" he asked.

"You might not have enough to spend this week, Max. Think about keeping your money in your wallet for next week. Saving money is important." I responded.

Max promptly ignored me and headed to his favorite stalls. The lady selling homemade popsicles charged $2.50 for a strawberry and cream popsicle. Max could not afford a popsicle with only $2.

Max then proceeded to the stand with chocolate zucchini bread where the price was $3 for a slice of bread. Max could not afford the bread.

He then moved to the lemonade stand where they sold large cups of lemonade for $4. Max also could not afford the lemonade.

"Mama, this isn't fair! I can't buy any of the things I want!" Max said.

"I realize this, Max. You really should consider saving your money until next week and working harder through the week so that you earn your full pay from the chore chart." I suggested.

"Just let me have the money, please, Mama," Max pleaded.

At this point, my inner-compassionate Mama wants to hand Max the money. I want him to enjoy the special treats that he has chosen to purchase. I want him to feel satisfaction from the $2 that he did earn that week. And I want him to be proud of himself for his accomplishments, albeit small ones. But I cannot do it.

"Max, you know there are no chore chart loans available. You can save your money until next week and work harder throughout the week." I answered.

Max's face fell to his chest as he began to cry in earnest, holding his little hands to his eyes.

Max was completely dejected over the situation. He wanted to spend his money immediately but did not have enough to spend on the items he wanted. We went home and Max was sad for about 15 minutes before he pulled out his Legos and started playing in the living room, the treats mostly forgotten.

"Mama, I did save my money for next week, but it made me sad." He told me later that afternoon.

Although Max was only six years old at the time, learning this lesson at six could be an incredible benefit. Instead of Max losing his house or car by overextending himself into debt as an adult, he could learn to save and not to overspend while the stakes are a popsicle and lemonade and not net worth. Watching Max hurt, seeing him upset and knowing that his little heart was breaking put me in a challenging situation. I wanted to bail him out by giving him the money to buy his treats. Knowing that a loan would backfire, I held out for a lesson learned early in life.

Narrative Writing Analysis

In this story, we see a tale of Max, the six year old boy who does not have enough money to buy the treats he wants and his mom who can choose to give him money to solve his problem or teach him a lesson that could last a lifetime. The audience is not specifically identified, but could be surmised by evaluating the publication. The tone is instructive yet charming. Every parent who has been in this situation knows how challenging it is to allow a child to learn a lesson the hard way. The purpose is to instruct and explain this parenting method.

The thesis statement is: In today's world, many parents succumb to a helicopter or hyper-protective parenting practice, which does not prepare children for an independent, responsible adulthood. The writer states the problem and its source by pointing out that some parents use a parenting style that is not effective. The writer also points out the effect of the problem, which is that this parenting method does not prepare children for adulthood.

The support which the writer employs is the story itself. She uses herself and her own personal experience to illustrate the point that some parenting practices are ineffective. She shows how Max tries to solve his problem but is unable to, how the mom is tempted to solve the problem for him and how Max realizes saving his money is a good idea in the end. The writer is also compassionate about making her point. Unlike persuasive writing, which tends to have a hard-hitting tone, this writer points out how difficult it is to teach children important lessons and how tempting it is to parent protectively.

Other support that the writer could have included might be: perhaps more detail on Max's perspective, a reflection on how Max became a great saver later in life or a comparison to a time the writer used the protective parenting method and it backfired on her. This piece could be used as an editorial, an advice column, an article in a parenting magazine or a blog posting. Its broad audience allows it to be applicable in different settings.

Example Compare or Contrast Short Answer

Compare or contrast two potential pets for your household.

I think that a cat would be a really good pet for our family. Right now, we have two small dogs but no cats. If we got a cat, the cat could sleep with my sister and that would make her happy. Getting a cat would be good for our whole family.

When I was born, my parents already had two dogs. These dogs are very small and very hyper. We have a Jack Russell Terrier and a Chihuahua. Both of these dogs bark all the time and sometimes wake us up. Although my parents love the dogs, the dogs are also annoying with all the barking. A cat would be calm and want to sleep and cuddle, so that would be really nice.

My sister is only four but she has always wanted a cat. She would like a cat to sleep with her and cuddle her because sometimes she has bad dreams. Also, she likes to play and the dogs run away from her so a cat would be good. Our whole family would like to have a cat, so we should get one.

Compare or Contrast Short Answer Analysis

In this short answer, we see just a couple of paragraphs that contrast cats and dogs. This young writer suggests that a cat would be a good addition to a home that already has two dogs. The audience might be a classroom teacher, the writer's parents or grandparents. The purpose is to explain the benefits of a cat by contrasting a cat's qualities against those of dogs.

The thesis statement is: I think that a cat would be a really good pet for our family. This young writer takes a mature stance when addressing the issue. No begging, pleading or irrational arguments here. This writer includes a valid, thoughtful viewpoint to present.

The support that a cat would be a good addition to this home includes: a cat would be interested in spending time with the little sister, a cat would comfort the little sister while sleeping, two dogs are already in the house and the cat would be calm where the dogs are not. This writer incorporates logical, caring support for the thesis statement, including the consideration for the little sister.

Other support that the writer could have brought up might include: a statement from the little sister about her wishes on getting a cat, pointing out the faults of the dogs which would not be a problem with the cat and the ease of maintenance and care of a cat. This short answer could work well as the content of an email or letter, it could be the text of a speech or it could be used as part of a brochure or presentation on cats as pets. The topic is broad enough to engage a wide audience of animal lovers.

Example Research Response

Construct a memo answering the research question: Should Americans work more or less? The United States may be the land of baseball, apple pie and freedom but its people are overworked and unhappy. Americans work more weekly hours than any other country, enjoy less vacation and struggle to provide the basic necessities of life. Other countries work harder to support their citizens and ensure a happier and healthier lifestyle. By working less, Americans could be happier.

The world's happiest people are spread across Northern Europe. Denmark, Finland, Sweden and Norway consistently rank high on the list of the world's happiest people. America ranks in the middle range of the happiness index. As well, Americans work an average of 47 hours per week, although many workers claim to work as much as 60 hours per week and more. Scandinavians typically work 38 hours per week, enjoy 6 weeks of paid annual vacation and are arguably the happiest people in the world.

Does all of this work pay off? Although some Americans find that their work equates to a higher standard of living, most do not. Current statistics show that the poverty rate in the United States is 34% and that only 30% of Americans are financially able to take an annual two week vacation. 67% of Americans claim that they work "too many hours per week" and another 52% claim they take work home after the work day ends.

The American economic system of people working long hours, going without vacation to relax and struggling to make ends meet has resulted in a culture of unhappy people. If Americans worked less and relaxed more, their quality of life and overall happiness would improve.

Research Writing Analysis

In this piece, we see the writer uses multiple statistics to answer the research question- Should Americans work more or less. The tone is expository because the writer is explaining the outcome of the research. The audience is not stated specifically but could relate to business owners, workers or policy makers in a variety of fields. The purpose is to explain the outcome of research.

The thesis statement is: The United States may be the land of baseball, apple pie and freedom but its people are overworked and unhappy. The writer acknowledges that there are many great elements of American life-baseball, apple pie and freedom. The problem is not in these areas but in the number of hours that Americans work. The writer suggests that the outcome of lacking free time is an overworked and unhappy populace.

The support is all in the statistics collected from research. The writer uses a comparison between Americans and Scandinavians to show three things: number of hours worked, amount of vacation time and happiness index. The writer also includes the average weekly hours that American workers work, how much more they work at home and how many work 60 or more hours per week. This data is compared against that of the Scandinavians. Finally, the writer uses outcome data to in this piece: poverty rate, standard of living and vacation time taken.

Other support that the writer could have brought up might include: more data on the subtopics of vacation time, work hours and happiness index. The writer could compare America against other cultures like Japan, China and the

United Kingdom. Also, including quotations, results from surveys and expert opinions would be useful in this piece.

Overall, this piece is a demonstration on how to construct an argument by starting with the researched data and constructing a thesis statement based on the data's outcome. This writing could be used as part of a larger piece like an essay, editorial or blog post. It could be included in a presentation like a brochure or broken into a power point or other presentation tool for a speech.

Conclusion

The purpose of *The Simple Guide to Thesis Statements and Support* is to help writers improve their writing skills. In this book, we covered what thesis statements are and different ways to write them. We also covered what makes up valid support for a thesis statement and how to construct it. Five full-length examples were given to illustrate how to write and support a thesis statement for both academic and professional style writing.

Most people spend time writing. Whether in the classroom, in the office, or at home, the majority of people need efficient writing skills so that they can get their ideas across easily and clearly. Being able to state and support a thesis statement can mean the difference between communicating clearly or coming off as confusing. Practice writing and supporting thesis statements for essays, memos and letters, and over time, your writing will improve. Writing is a skill that requires practice and ongoing development for most people to master.

Sincerely, we hope that after reading this book that your confidence in writing and supporting viewpoints has improved. Writing is a lifelong process and no one is born a perfect writer. It is a skill that requires practice and continuing improvement to perfect.

Good Luck With Your Writing!

Glossary

A

APA: (American Psychological Association) a writing format and style associated and created for the writing and citation of books and academic papers in the behavioral and social sciences

adolescent: a young person in the process of developing from a child into an adult

academics: belonging to or related to a place of learning such as a college or an academy

Alcott, Louisa May: (1832-1888) an American novelist and poet best known for the novel Little Women (1868)

American Civil War: (1861-1865) a civil war in the America fought between seven (eventually eleven) Confederate slave states and the remainder of the United States. The war began with the secession of the Southern states from the Union of the United States.

analysis: a detailed examination of the essential parts or structure of something

anecdote: a short interesting or amusing story about an actual person or event

Angelou, Maya: (1928-2014) an American author, poet, actress and dancer best known for her series of autobiographies

arguable opinion: a viewpoint or position in a thesis statement that can be defended and supported

argument: a reason given with the intention to persuade others toward a truth or falsehood

assessment: the evaluation of a student's abilities

B

Bell and Trust: a fictitious financial institution invented by the author

bias: being in favor of or against a certain thing, group or person compared with another, usually in an unfair manner

Bibliography: a list of books or writings related to a certain subject or used by an author in certain work

block format method: a format of paragraph writing where the writer focuses each paragraph on one topic or one point and exhausts all of the details about that point before moving on

blog: a website or web page designed as a forum for a person or group's opinion; an online journal

body paragraphs: the main portion of an essay that supports or proves the thesis statement

book reflection: an essay written about a book with the subject matter being the personal feelings, suggested improvements and perspective of a book

brainstorm: the act of considering or investigating a subject to solve a problem or generate ideas

C

Car Owner Magazine: a fictitious automobile magazine created by the author

Centers for Disease Control: a federal agency in the United States who's main goal is to protect public health through the control and prevention of disease

Chicago: a writing format and style widely used in publishing in the United States

chronological: to arrange in order of occurrence

cite: to quote or refer to a book or author as an authority, proof or example

colleague: someone who works in the same organization as you

commentary: an ongoing spoken accompaniment to a broadcast, film or sporting event

communicable: can be passed from one person or animal to another

compose: to write or create something

concisely: expressed using only a few words yet easily understandable

conclusion paragraph: the ending paragraph to a piece of writing that should wrap up the entire composition

conjecture: an opinion or conclusion based on incomplete information

connotations: an idea or feeling that a word invokes in addition to its normal meaning

contrast: the action of calling attention to notable differences

D

Davis, Kim: county clerk in Morehead, Kentucky (2015) who refused to issue any marriage licenses to same sex couples regardless of court orders

documentary: a media form using pictures, video footage and interviews with people to provide a factual report

draft: a plan, writing, letter or drawing that may have or require changes prior to being finished

E

editorial: a newspaper or magazine article in which the editor gives their opinion on a current event

emphasis: special importance or attention given to one thing in particular

essay: a short composition on a single subject usually reflecting the author's viewpoint

expository: written with the intention to explain or describe something

F

FBI: (Federal Bureau of Investigation) is the domestic intelligence, security service and federal law enforcement service in the United States

formal: following correct official methods and rules of something

format: the arrangement or organization of something

foreshadowing: to provide some inkling of a future event especially in writing

G

graduate: a degree in education after one has already earned an earlier degree such as a Master's degree

H

Hemingway, Ernest: (1899-1961) American author and journalist, he is most famous for *The Old Man in the Sea* for which he won the Nobel Prize for literature

Hierarchal: classified into levels or layers by various criteria

hook statement: the first one or two sentences of an essay designed to grab the intended reader's attention

Hughes, Langston: (1902-1967) an American poet, social activist, novelist and playwright, best known as the leader of the Harlem Renaissance

hypothesis: an idea that attempts to explain something but has not yet been proved or tested

I

Infographic: a visual chart or diagram used to represent an idea, information, concept or data

infuse: to put in or cause to be filled with something

interoffice communications: the communications within the offices of a company or organization

innate: something existing in a person or thing that is natural, not learned or added; instinctive

J

Jewell, Richard: (1962-2007) American police officer who became famous in connection with the Centennial Olympic Park bombing at the 1996 Olympics in Georgia. He was later found to be completely innocent.

L

Labor Party: a political party representing the interests of the ordinary working people

legislature: people who are elected to create laws in a certain area

M

MLA: a writing style and format typically used in scholarly works and student research papers

N

narrative: characterized by the telling of a story

National Parks: areas of land protected by a government body for the appreciation and use by the people

New Yorker: a weekly published periodical containing commentary and reporting on: politics, international affairs, popular culture and the arts, science and technology, and business, along with fiction, poetry, humor, and cartoons.

Norden, Lake: a fictitious place invented by the author

novice: someone who is in the beginning stages of learning a subject or skill

O

O'Dell, Susan: a fictitious person invented by the author

organic: related to food grown without synthetic fertilizers or pesticides

opinion: the attitude, thoughts or viewpoint of a person or group

opinion statement: *see thesis statement*

P

paragraph: a section of writing that begins on a new line and contains one or more sentences on a particular theme or topic

persuasive: having the ability to get or convince others to do something

piece: a single instance of a particular thing or type

political pundit: an actual or pretended expert in politics who gives opinion or criticism on policy or politicians usually with heavy bias

pose: to put something forward, assert or ask

preface: an introduction to a book or other writing

prompt: to inspire or cause an action

proposal: a plan or suggestion put forward for consideration

proposition statement: *see thesis statement*

publishing: the act of making information available for everyone to read

Q

quotation: a phrase taken from another person especially to support a point or argument

R

rephrase: to say or write the same thing only using different words

resume': a document describing a person's education, skills, experience and qualifications used when applying for work

rhetorical question: asked in order to cause an effect or make a statement rather than actually answering the question

S

sentence: a string of words intended to express a statement, instruction or question and will typically have a subject and a verb. A written sentence will start with a capitol letter and end with a period, question mark or exclamation.

Sherman, Katy: a fictitious person invented by the author

skimming: reading through materials in a quick manner while looking for specific information

standardized test: the same test given in the same manner to all test takers typically in the education system with the attempt to evaluate students, curriculum and teaching staff

standpoint: *see thesis statement*

support: to prove that a statement is true or correct

support statement: *see thesis statement*

T

thematic: relating to the idea, subject or theme

theory: an idea that attempts to explain how or why something happens

thesis: an idea, theory or opinion used to explain something

thesis statement: a statement, usually short that summarizes the main point or opinion of a piece of writing, such as an essay or research paper

Thoreau, Henry David: (1817-1862) American author, poet, abolitionist, philosopher, and naturalist; best known for his book *Walden*

topic: the subject written or spoken about

transition: the process of changing from one condition or situation to another

Turabian: a writing style and format designed to be used for research papers

U

unifying statement: *see thesis statement*

W

Walker Alice: (1944-) American author and activist best known for her critically acclaimed novel *The Color Purple* for which she won the Pulitzer Prize

writing process: a series of steps a writer would follow to record experiences, observations, data and research

Works Cited: the part of a paper or project where all of the sources used to write the paper are listed

Index

D

E

F

H

I

N

O

P

Q

R

S

Afterward

Thank you for reading *The Simple Guide to Thesis Statements and Support*. Please feel free to reach out to the author, Patricia Martin, through the publisher, On Demand Instruction, through the links below.

Subscribe to the On Demand Instruction Writing Center's blog for free resources and giveaways at:

Ondemandinstruction.net

Also, sign up for updates and giveaways from the full line of Simple Guide Books, including the upcoming *The Simple Guide to The Writing Process*, *The Simple Guide to The Research Process* and *The Simple Guide for Successful Virtual Students* from On Demand Instruction at:

Ondemandinstruction.com

If you enjoyed this book and found it helpful, please leave a review at the store from where you purchased it.

Acknowledgements

Writing is painfully hard work for me. None of it comes naturally and I fail a million times before I get one thing right. From the bottom of my soul thank you to James Stefon, Stephanie Weber, Karina Doyle and Corrine Jacobs for the reading, editing and reassuring. Your encouragement has been a blessing.

Thank you for the decades of writing teachers who shared their wisdom, Dr. Polly Palmer, Linda Bendorf and Jo Kadlecek in particular, who nagged, edited, pushed, pestered and cheered novice writers to keep going. Your voices are the ones I hear when I close my eyes and listen to my heart.

And thank you eternally to Jason. For everything.

Inforgraphics created using **easel.ly**

Videos created using **screencast-o-matic.com**

About the Author

Patricia Martin MA, MEd is a writer and secondary teacher. Ms. Martin earned a Master's degree in Writing and Communication from Regis University and a Master's degree in Educational Leadership from Adams State University. Ms. Martin believes that learning is the finest way people can develop themselves and better their lives. Her own writing process is one of continuous learning and improvement. Most of her time is spent writing, teaching and raising her two children. She lives near Boulder, CO with her family.

Made in the USA
Middletown, DE
13 February 2016